My Memories of John Hartford

American Made Music Series

My Memories of

JOHN
HARTFORD

BOB CARLIN

University Press of Mississippi / Jackson

The University Press of Mississippi is the scholarly publishing agency of
the Mississippi Institutions of Higher Learning: Alcorn State University,
Delta State University, Jackson State University, Mississippi State University,
Mississippi University for Women, Mississippi Valley State University,
University of Mississippi, and University of Southern Mississippi.

www.upress.state.ms.us

The University Press of Mississippi is a member
of the Association of University Presses.

Library of Congress Cataloging-in-Publication Data

Names: Carlin, Bob, author.
Title: My memories of John Hartford / Bob Carlin.
Other titles: American made music series.
Description: Jackson : University Press of Mississippi, 2024. | Series:
American made music series | Includes bibliographical references and index.
Identifiers: LCCN 2023056459 (print) | LCCN 2023056460 (ebook) | ISBN
9781496851383 (hardback) | ISBN 9781496851390 (trade paperback) | ISBN
9781496851406 (epub) | ISBN 9781496851413 (epub) | ISBN 9781496851420
(pdf) | ISBN 9781496851437 (pdf)
Subjects: LCSH: Hartford, John. | Bluegrass musicians—United
States—Biography. | Bluegrass musicians—United States—Anecdotes. |
Singers—United States—Biography. | Fiddlers—United States—Biography.
| Banjoists—United States—Biography.
Classification: LCC ML419.H3415 C37 2024 (print) | LCC ML419.H3415
(ebook) | DDC 782.42162/130092—dc23/eng/20240105
LC record available at https://lccn.loc.gov/2023056459
LC ebook record available at https://lccn.loc.gov/2023056460

British Library Cataloging-in-Publication Data available

For my son, Benjamin, who, as a child, listened to more than his share of John Hartford's music. As a result, Ben memorized the *Good Old Boys* album, inspiring his goal of being asked to sing the title track onstage with the Hartford Stringband.

Contents

PREFACE AND THANKS IX

CHAPTER ONE: I'm Glad You Didn't Know Me Back Then 3

CHAPTER TWO: The Master of High Laconic 28

CHAPTER THREE: We Just Got Back from Japan. 49

CHAPTER FOUR: I Could Always Do This Show without You . . . 83

CHAPTER FIVE: You Certainly Are Easily Entertained,
and for That, I Am Eternally Grateful. 103

EPILOGUE: Afterlife: When It's Over, It's Just Over 135

SELECTED BIBLIOGRAPHY 139

SELECTED DISCOGRAPHY: John Hartford and Bob Carlin 141

INDEX 143

Preface and Thanks

Don't get famous for something you don't like to do. I do what's in my heart and if it works, that's great. If it doesn't work, at least I haven't wasted my time. If I didn't do what was in my heart, the worst thing that would happen is that I'd be successful and I'd have to do it again. It would be awful to be successful at something that I didn't enjoy doing.

—JOHN HARTFORD

[John] Hartford is one of the most protean, creative, and uncategorizable figures on the American music scene. . . . The more time has passed, in fact, the more remarkable and significant a figure he appears to be.

Hartford was eclectic before eclecticism was a trend. His deep knowledge of, and passion for, traditional music never stood in the way of his creative curiosity, and vice versa. His fascinating recordings, beginning in the late 1960s, have consistently broken-down stylistic divisions between folk music, country, bluegrass, rock and pop. . . .

He has refused to accept any limitations, or definitions of himself and who he should be, or where he should put his talents. He has always insisted on being himself, which has meant being many things.

—TOM PIAZZA, BOOKLET NOTES, *GOOD OLD BOYS*

As I write this preface, more than twenty years have elapsed since the passing of songwriter and musician John Hartford. My friendship and working relationship with John dates to August 23, 1985. On that Friday, I interviewed him for the local broadcast of *Fresh Air* with Terry Gross on WHYY-FM, the National Public Radio affiliate in Philadelphia, Pennsylvania. As I remember it, I was asked to converse with John by Andy Braunfeld of the Philadelphia Folksong Society, which organized an annual event where John was appearing.

Throughout his short life, John was a hit tunesmith ("Gentle on My Mind"), television star (*The Smothers Brothers Comedy Hour, The Glen Campbell Goodtime Hour*), godfather of newgrass music, festival headliner, multiple Grammy-winning recording artist (on labels including RCA Victor, Warner Bros, Flying Fish, Rounder, and Small Dog) and movie soundtrack creator (*O Brother, Where Are Thou?* and *Down from the Mountain*, both by the Coen brothers). During that time, Hartford appealed (and continues to appeal after his passing) to a wide audience of musicians, concertgoers, music consumers, and television viewers.

When we formally met, John had already lived many of these multiple lives and through numerous phases of his musical career. However, at that time, John was still considered a big star who sold out large auditoriums with his one-man show.

By then, John had settled into a comfortable existence living on the Cumberland River outside of Nashville, Tennessee. He was often on television, toured throughout the country as it pleased him, and piloted the steamboat *Julia Belle Swain* during the summer.

Although this was the first time I'd had a conversation with John, his music had held my attention for the prior fifteen-plus years. I'd discovered John's RCA albums in the late 1960s, when, while still in high school, I began working in radio. His *Aereo-Plain* record for Warner Bros., of which I still own an original vinyl LP, was a major influence on my own musical development. Commencing with the 1970 Philadelphia Folk Festival, after my own modest career as a performer had lurched to a start, I used to see John from afar at the events where we were both appearing. Because John was a headliner, and I was far down on the bill, I never jammed with John nor dreamt of approaching him to initiate a dialogue. Nor, honestly, because of how I initially viewed John's performances (gimmicky and thin on substance), was I interested in John after the 1971 release of *Aereo-Plain*. I only began to reevaluate his music in the early 1980s, when players whom I respected such as Robin and Linda Williams began challenging my critiques.

Therefore, given my history as an observer of John's music, I was surprised, and pleasantly so, when John openly gave in-depth responses to my questions. I found him inquisitive and knowledgeable about the history of bluegrass music, as well as an intelligent observer of the human condition. Well aware of my position in showbiz's pecking order (low down in the hierarchy), I was taken aback (in a good way) when John closed the interview with "[I] enjoy your banjo playing, keep it up." He also told me during the program that he was "a big fan" of my music.

My reassessment of John Hartford was complete.

From this meeting over microphones developed a sixteen-year affiliation. For the first five years of our acquaintance, I would visit with John when touring schedules placed us in the same locales: when we were both traveling for our music; I was gigging or teaching in the Nashville area; his performances brought him near my home; or, between those times, by telephone (these were the pre-internet/pre-cellphone days). I should note that I was not the only person with whom John maintained this type of friendship. Rather, relationships like ours were a common part of John's life throughout the whole time that we were associates.

Six years into our friendship, a working collaboration developed between John and me. I first accompanied him on several albums, eventually becoming his project manager for audio and video recordings. Finally, I was recruited into John's last Stringband, for which I also was the de facto road manager and right-hand guy.

Years after our initial meeting, I wondered if John would have welcomed my advances when our paths first crossed. Whenever John and I would discuss the 1970s, he would often remark, "I'm glad you didn't know me back then. You wouldn't have liked me very much; I was a real S.O.B."

Why do I think John and I became friends and musical partners? For one thing, we had a lot in common. John and I were both born in New York City. Our parents followed the arts. Each of us had a parent who was a painter. Both sets of our fathers and mothers folk danced and square danced. Our fathers were scientists with similar personalities. John and I, encouraged by our families, played music from a young age and were avid readers. We both had an interest in radio, and pursued broadcasting before becoming professional musicians.

John and I obviously diverged when it came to choosing our musical paths. A few years ahead of me, John left behind traditional playing styles to take advantage of opportunities down a more commercial route. I hewed closer to traditional forms and attempted to make folk music palatable to the largest audience possible. Therefore, John achieved much greater desirability and profitability within the larger entertainment industry than I ever could or would.

I begin this book with several segments covering the years before our friendship. The pages that follow those sections detail the last fifteen years of John Hartford's life. Included are in-depth descriptions of John's lifestyle, as well as his philosophies about music, performing, recording, and living as he expressed them to me or to those around him, with some road stories thrown in for good measure. Those last fifteen years of his short life, tempered by available information, are viewed here through the impressionist lenses of my own experience.

This has not been an easy book to write. With my father's passing in 1996, John became, in some manner, a surrogate parent. When John died in 2001, it was if I had to relive the loss of my father in addition to the departure of a good friend.

Luckily, John and I both shared a trait—which he put it into a song, "I Can't Stand to Throw Anything Away"—that aided in the writing of this book. These materials included calendar books as well as recording session tapes and notes. Newspapers.com was useful in assembling a Hartford timeline that especially aided in reconstructing John's career. I also had help from and thank Art Menius; Chris Sharp, Mike Compton, and Matt Combs of the Hartford Stringband; my wife, Rachel Smith, who experienced many of these memories with me; Jamie Harford and Katie and Eric Harford Hogue of the John Hartford Estate; johnhartford.com; Richard Carlin and David Alff, editors supreme; Tom Piazza; Chris Coole; Matt Neiburger; the Steam Powered Preservation Society; Gail Gillespie and *The Old Time Herald*; Rounder Records; Dan Levenson; Danny Miller of *Fresh Air*; and Martin Fisher and Greg Reish at the Center for Popular Music of Middle Tennessee State University. However, only I bear the responsibility for this work; it is entirely of my own making.

> *Now, here's to all them Good Old Boys.*
> *Cheer 'em on, make a lot of noise*
> —"GOOD OLD BOYS"

My Memories of John Hartford

CHAPTER ONE

I'm Glad You Didn't Know Me Back Then

On the Cumberland River, where the muddy waters flow
Lived an old riverman that played the banjo
He wore a derby hat so everyone would know
His show had come to town
—Matt Combs and Bob Carlin, "John, Bring That Fiddle 'Round"

John Cowan Harford (the "t" was a later addition) was born in New York City on December 30, 1937. From an aristocratic family, John was the descendant of business owners on his father's side and politicians and creative types on his mother's (through whom he was related to the playwright Tennessee Williams).

John's parents had moved east from St. Louis to complete his father's medical education. Dr. Carl Gayler Harford and family then returned to the Gateway to the West in order, one assumes, to be closer to family. Once back in the city on the Mississippi River, Dr. Harford began private practice, and two more children, both daughters, followed. By John's teenage years, Carl Harford had joined the faculty of Washington University, the alma mater for both of John's parents.

John's mother, Mary Broadhead Cowan, had trained as an occupational therapist. Stories about his upbringing describe John, possibly because he was the eldest and the only male child, as the sibling most favored by his mother. John enjoyed being the center of attention, an attribute that later would serve him well as an entertainer.

Mary was an avid painter and took most of the responsibility for nurturing the artistic talents of her only son. Toward those ends, John drew from an early age, read voraciously, and acted with the local children's theater group.

As a child of privilege raised within a gated community, John attended the private Community School for elementary grades. His junior and senior high school years were completed at the progressive John Burroughs School, where, among other activities, he competed on the tennis team.

Well, the first time I heard Earl Scruggs, I was listenin' to the radio
I fell out of bed, and I bounced off all the four walls
—"On the Radio"

By his mid-teens, John had come under the influence of bluegrass and folk music. When I interviewed him in 1985 for the *Fresh Air* radio program, I asked John about how he started playing bluegrass music. John's memories came out in a slow torrent of words:

My mom and dad square danced, and I used to hear fiddle music [at those dances]. And I always liked that kind of music. We [also] used to listen to the Grand Ole Opry on Saturday night, the Prince Albert [sponsored] portion. It would come through [the radio] and we'd hear Stringbean [Dave Akeman] play the banjo. And there [also] was an old man [that] lived near us named Dr. Gray who played an old two-finger style. He played stuff like "Green Corn" and "The Preacher and the Bear."

I had a great-uncle who played the mandolin and there was an old mandolin laying around my grandmother's house. I played on that. And then my grandfather had a fiddle that he played when he was young. He used to keep it in the closet under the coats. And I was told not to mess with it. [However,] I used to crawl into the coat closet on my stomach and get the fiddle bow out and put it down on the fiddle strings and pull it back and forth [to] where nobody could hear it.

But I loved the banjo [most of all] and I wanted to play. So, my mother and I found an old banjo on top of a pile of junk at the Goodwill store and bought that. I got it strung up and tried to imitate a five-string on a four-string [instrument] for a year or so. And then we figured out how to drill a hole in the side of the neck and I put this little thumb peg in there and we converted this old plectrum banjo to a five-string. And that was my first five-string banjo.

The young John's watershed musical moment, as he often told it, occurred at a music park north of St. Louis. The Chain of Rocks grove was home to Roy Queen's Jamboree, where Roy would host the touring stars of country music.

Roy Queen had held forth over area radio for more than twenty years. As "The Lone Cowboy Singer," he initially performed over powerhouse KMOX ("Missouri Xmas Eve," named for when the station first signed on in 1925). Except for a brief sojourn to Cincinnati's WLW, Queen stayed continuously with KMOX from 1931 through 1947. Gradually moving into the role of disc jockey and announcer, by 1953 Roy was spinning records over KXLW and plugging the shows he was promoting at his Jamboree. Since Queen was also appearing with his band at local events, the Harford family may have learned about Roy's broadcasts and promotions through their interest in square dancing.

Listening to Roy Queen on the radio one day, John discovered that he would be bringing Grand Ole Opry stars Lester Flatt and Earl Scruggs and the Foggy Mountain Boys, including Benny Martin on the fiddle, to St. Louis. The fifteen-year-old aspiring musician, too young to hold a driving license, pestered his mother into taking him to the event. John later described that moment of first hearing Flatt & Scruggs live as akin to "being struck by lightning." As John recounted to me in 1985:

In about 1953, we had a local disc jockey around St. Louis named Roy Queen and he had a show [in] St. Louis and also on [a] Warrenton, Missouri, [radio station] for a furniture company. And [Roy] had a hillbilly park up on the Mississippi River and he kept announcing this group Flatt & Scruggs. One morning, he played this record [by them] called "Dear Old Dixie" and I about came out of my skin. I always loved the five-string banjo, but I'd never heard a banjo played like that. And I wasn't quite old enough to drive yet. So, my mother and I and a neighbor boy went up and heard this band. It was Lester and Earl and Benny Martin and Curly Seckler and Kentucky Slim [aka Charles Elza] on the bass. It turned out it was the last show that they did before they went to Nashville to do their first early morning Martha White 5:45 in the morning radio show [which occurred in June 1953]. That experience changed me forever.

From then onward, John would pattern his fiddling on Benny Martin and his banjo playing on that of Earl Scruggs.

Soon afterward, John and a friend rode the bus from St. Louis to Nashville, Tennessee, for his first outing to the Music City. The pair attended the Friday and Saturday night live broadcasts of the Grand Ole Opry. As John later recalled in "The Boys From North Carolina," his musical tribute to Earl Scruggs, "They stood in line, around the block / right back here at the Ryman / to hear that lick, that old mule kick / from the boy from North Carolina." John and his companion also stopped at the Ernest Tubb Record Shop on lower Broadway to purchase bluegrass recordings and watch the Midnight Jamboree that followed the Saturday Opry broadcast. During another particularly memorable trip to Nashville, John interviewed Earl Scruggs for the banjoist's fan club newsletter. Afterward, he finagled a ride with Scruggs to the Ryman Auditorium, then the home of the Opry. That first encounter would grow into a deep friendship between Hartford and Scruggs, and John was able to provide emotional support for the banjoist during some particularly tough periods in Earl's life.

John later discussed his early attraction to bluegrass music with journalist Robert K. Oermann of the *Tennessean* (November 27, 1983, 27):

The people who were my idols were [the] fiddlers and banjo pickers around home. And of the people that I heard on record and radio who really set me on fire—Bill Monroe, Benny Martin, Flatt & Scruggs—they were like people who worked at a trade. That regularity appealed to me.

By age eighteen, John was playing with his cousins Kate and Stoner Haven, with whom he attended the Burroughs school, in a group they named the Missouri Ridge Runners. This band performed at the National Folk Festival when the traveling event visited St. Louis. It's possible that John's song "First Girl I Loved," which he recorded in 1971 for the *Aereo-Plain* album, was inspired by his relationship with these cousins.

During the same period, John made the acquaintance of the musical Dillard family: banjoist Douglas, his younger brother/guitarist Rodney, and their father, fiddler Homer. John recalled those times for writer Art Menius:

> I think I was a senior in high school or in my first year at college when I met Douglas [at] a Lee Mace show with the Ozark Opry in St. Clair, Missouri. We started hanging around together around St. Louis [and playing music]. Rodney was going to high school in Salem, and he used to come [when visiting St. Louis] and sit in [on our music sessions].

Sometime before the beginning of 1958, John procured his first reel-to-reel tape recorder, a monaural machine made by the Wollensak company. Despite its Germanic-sounding name, this was an American-made pre-digital rig. The Wollensak was an institutional mainstay because of its solid construction and dependability. Although heavy and bulky, it *was* portable, and John began hauling it around to record the various fiddlers he had befriended.

Even though John mostly made these recordings as a learning aid, his documentary efforts helped insure the survival of the playing of these musicians. The transfer of John's early tapes to digital in the late 1990s by Jim Nelson, a St. Louis musician and librarian, instigated the recording of *Hamilton Ironworks*, John's last studio recording, which provided a tribute to his musical beginnings.

Gradually, bluegrass and fiddle music took over John's life. But, with his parents concerned about John's ability to support himself, he had to come up with a path forward that they would accept. As he told me at WHYY in 1985:

My dad was a doctor and a professor, and it was always assumed that I would go to college. But I had an artistic bent and I wasn't very good at following books. And, so, I went a couple of years studying fine arts. I've always been able to draw and paint, but I never really had it in my mind to do that [for my livelihood].

After leaving Washington University in 1960, a year shy of earning his bachelor of fine arts degree, John worked for a period as a commercial artist. Even after he had abandoned this career path, John maintained a solid interest in art, sketching throughout the remainder of his life. John had a particularly strong focus on illustration, nurtured by his lifelong exposure to the drawings in the *New Yorker* magazine. He often befriended professional cartoonists such as Jim Scancarelli and Dan Martin. These relationships led to fiddler Scancarelli including John as a recurring character in a series of 1991 *Gasoline Alley* newspaper strips. Martin also drew John, producing his "Weatherbird" character for the *St. Louis Post-Dispatch* dressed to resemble John playing his banjo. John thought enough of Martin to write the fiddle tunes "Weatherbird Reel" and "The Wife of Dan Weatherbird" in his honor. (See *John Hartford's Mammoth Collection of Fiddle Tunes*, 2018.)

Besides art and music, John was passionate about the boats that traveled up and down the Mississippi River.

As a child, John had dreamed of piloting riverboats and spent a goodly amount of time gazing at photographs of historic vessels in local libraries. Later in his life, he would often credit this interest to a past life living and/or working on the Mississippi River.

Now I had a teacher when I went to school,
she loved the river and she taught about it, too
I was a pretty bad boy, but she called my bluff
With her great big collection of steamboat stuff, oh yeah
—"Miss Ferris"

Another early influence on John's attraction to river travel was Miss Ruth Ferris (1891–1993), his fourth-grade teacher at the Community School. A steamboat aficionado and historian, Ferris inspired the young John Hartford to subscribe to the *Waterways Journal*, the official organ for river folk. Ruth and John maintained a relationship throughout their lives. The Hartford and Ferris correspondence can be read at the St. Louis Mercantile Library at the University of Missouri-St. Louis, which houses both individuals' river collections.

At WHYY, John told me about how he was almost drawn into a nautical career:

> I've always loved boats and at a very early age, I started riding the old paddle wheel steamboats out of St. Louis. And, when I turned fifteen, I started working on the river in the summers. So, by the time I was going to college, I was working every summer on the river. And, I had assumed that, at some point, if I could slither out, I'd go full time on the river. And I was headed in my mind to[ward] becom[ing] a boat pilot.

Even though fifteen was underage, John talked his way into a position as night watchman on the steamboat *Delta Queen*. Subsequently, John spent his summers as a deckhand on Mississippi River barges.

However, the pull of music proved too strong for his other career choices as either an artist or a riverboat pilot. John related to me:

> I had played music all this time, but I never considered that it was something that you could do for a living. And I got off the river just toward the end of one summer and went to work playing fiddle in a South St. Louis dance hall. And I never went back on the river [for a long time after that].

In one of the many interviews with the *St. Louis Post-Dispatch*, his hometown newspaper ("Hartford: Riverboats and Music," July 20, 1978), John discussed these beginnings for his professional career in music. John started out playing for square dances at Compton Hall, at the corner of Compton and Park. He remembered:

> A woman named Diddie Woolsey ran it. For a while I [also] played fiddle and worked with a house band for radio station WEW [the city's oldest radio broadcaster; during the time

John was employed there, the station hosted a country and western format]. In East St. Louis I played with Curly Nelson and with Fiddlin' Willie in St. Louis. Doug Dillard, Marvin and Clifford Hawthorne, and I were in a band together [as well].

John's first "professional" musical group included Norman Ford and Don Brown. With John on the banjo, the Ozark Mountain Trio, as this bluegrass-style assembly was named, hosted a local television show. They also recorded two singles for Marlo Records released in 1961, as well as a four-song EP titled *Backwoods Gospel Songs* on Shannon Records, issued in 1962. (Both have been reissued on *Backroads, Rivers & Memories*, Real Gone Music.)

Fortunately, as things worked out, and knowing how difficult it would be to make his living as a bluegrass musician, John ultimately chose to pursue a job as a radio disc jockey. This would allow him to keep his hand in music, as many small radio stations still hosted live programming. John could also continue to perform in his spare time.

John began deejaying at KTSL in St. Louis, and moved to WHOW in Clinton, Illinois, at the end of July 1963, where he stayed through most of 1964. John's deejaying career then took him to Memphis and, finally, Nashville.

In our 1985 conversation for *Fresh Air*, I asked John about his time in broadcasting, and he described the world of small-town radio that he had entered:

I worked at WHOW in Clinton, Illinois, for a while. I'd sign on about 5:45 in the morning and do the news and then we'd [play] some records and had a little live show. Sometimes we'd do it live and sometimes we'd put it on tape the day before. And then I think about ten o'clock in the morning, we had a guy that would come in for fifteen minutes, he owned a car lot there in town. And he had a guitar. He'd put a copy of *Country Song Roundup* up on the rack and he'd sing a few songs out of that and sell cars. We did a lot of what they called "per inquiry," "P.I." things, where you actually were paid by the amount of mail that you could pull for the ads that you [read]. We plugged products such as Gypsy Fish Bait Lure and Royal Jelly and the amazing towels. . . .

The main thing I remember was, [in a radio announcer's exaggerated voice] "if you get your order postmarked by midnight tomorrow night, you'll get a coupon entitling you to have a roll of film developed and printed absolutely free of charge."

Then, I went to [stations in] Fulton, Missouri [possibly KFAL], and Malden, Missouri [KMAL?], and moved from there to Nashville. I [really] went down [to Nashville] to get into the music business, but I started [out] in radio. Eventually, I phased out of [radio work] and [went to playing] music full time.

In 1963, while still a disc jockey, John met and married singer Betty L. Beck (born circa 1935), and the two performed together on some of the regional Midwestern radio stations where John was employed. The couple would eventually have two children. James Cowan "Jamie" (born 1965) became a musician and performed with his father in the late 1980s and early 1990s. His younger sister, Kathryn Gayler "Katie," was born four years later. Jamie and Katie now control the John Hartford estate.

A GUY CAN STARVE TO DEATH JUST AS EASILY IN NASHVILLE AS ANYWHERE ELSE, AND HAVE MORE FUN DOING IT.

By 1965, John had been hired by WSIX radio in Nashville, Tennessee. Around the same time, the Glaser brothers Tompall, Chuck, and Jim recruited him to write songs for their publishing company. Songwriting was a key component to his eventually leaving radio behind. In our interview, John explained to me what had led him to attempt composing popular songs:

I'm gonna confess, I originally started [writing songs] because I knew that—and I wasn't really a singer per se—[in order] to get jobs and to work as a professional musician, I needed to do more than [just] play the banjo. Most of the music jobs that I had I was able to get because I would double on fiddle. And some of them, I would play lead guitar; I'd play banjo licks on the guitar. I really loved the banjo, but the banjo was considered a novelty instrument.

My two big influences were Earl Scruggs and Benny Martin. And Earl just stands there and plays the banjo. Benny, who was the fiddle player in that early Flatt & Scruggs band [that I heard as a teenager], does everything. He plays the fiddle, he plays the guitar, he plays the mandolin, he sings, and he writes songs. He's a complete show unto himself. And I think the influence of Benny Martin put me to writing songs. I realized that I needed to do more than just play the banjo and the fiddle.

[After] I got into writing songs, it became really enjoyable for me, and I became consumed with it. But it wasn't something that I had started out to do, it was something I stumbled into.

A year after moving to the Music City, musician and record producer Chet Atkins heard John's composition "Eve of My Multiplication," a song referencing the birth of his first child. Thinking he had found another Bob Dylan, Chet signed John to a recording contract with RCA Victor. It was Atkins who added the "t" to make John a "Hartford," noting something to the effect that "everyone would call him that anyway." Chet assigned the newly christened John Hartford to staff producer Felton Jarvis, who would oversee all of John's Nashville projects (Rick Jarrard would supervise the three discs cut in California). Between 1966 and 1970, John would make seven LPs for RCA Records, all but one officially released during those years.

Obviously, with each succeeding recording, more new John Hartford songs entered his performing repertoire. Ones that survived throughout his career were the mouth sounds novelty "(Good Old Electric) Washing Machine" (*Earthwords & Music*), as well as the observational "The Six O'Clock Train and a Girl with Green Eyes" and "I Would Not Be Here" (*The Love Album*). When his RCA recordings all went out of print, John began recycling the material recorded for that label on his newly made platters. These included the love song "No End of Love" from *Earthwords & Music* (the title song for a 1996 collection) and *Housing Project*'s apocalyptical "I'm Still Here" for *Gum Tree Canoe* (Flying Fish Records, 1984).

John's compositions of the 1960s are quite different from his "mature" songs composed during his middle age. These initial stream-of-consciousness "word movies," as he was to characterize them, jammed a lot more lyrics and imagery into each line. The chord progressions and melodies as well differed from those later in his career. The songs on the initial RCA releases often were built around minor keys, as John leaned toward similar melodies based around descending changes. There is a toughness and even grittiness to these songs, what Chuck Glaser, when asked to describe John's approach, termed "realism" in Glaser's notes to *The Love Album* (RCA Victor, 1968). The requirement to fill two albums a year with original creations lasted for at least the first two years of his RCA Victor contract. John once told me that he eventually wrote on autopilot, falling back on formulas to produce the twelve songs necessary every six months.

This sudden move from playing in bluegrass bands to performing as a solo singer-songwriter required quite an adjustment. In his new role, John told Art Menius:

> I played a little bit on the fiddle and a little bit on the guitar and the banjo, but mostly I just sat there and sang my weird songs. I was really into being a singer-songwriter in those days, so I did these long introspective songs [that] I wrote.

Eventually, John would grow into a consummate entertainer, charming his way into mainstream popularity.

Although much of his songwriting output was to prove popular only with his own audiences, one song, "Gentle on My Mind," was extensively covered in hit versions by other performers. In an oft-repeated story, John explained to me on *Fresh Air* how he came to create his best-known composition:

> It was written in a period when I was writing four or five songs a day, and my aim was to fill up the tapes. I wasn't taking what I was doing seriously, which is probably why I was able to write [the songs]. I worked at [WSIX] and I knew if I could take Chuck Glaser a tape the next morning, I'd have his attention.

Therefore, I'd sit at the radio station in the evening and do the news during drive time. Then, when that was done, I ran a show from ten until midnight, which was what they called easy listening, and write lyrics. And then I'd go home. Before I'd go to bed, I'd crank up the tape recorder and I'd put these lyrics [I'd just written] up [on a music stand], get my banjo out and just make up these melodies and put them on tape. And then I'd get up the next morning and take the tape down to Chuck Glaser.

During the time described above, Chuck would later remember John bringing in weekly tapes containing six to fifteen new original songs.

"Gentle on My Mind" was a very oblique love song composed after seeing the movie *Doctor Zhivago*, released in 1965. John told me that, at the time, he thought "it was just another song." In fact, "Gentle" was an unusual composition, and an unlikely smash, because it lacked a chorus and, therefore, a curious candidate for radio play in the late 1960s.

Originally a hit for Glen Campbell, "Gentle" was eventually covered by everyone from Aretha Franklin to Elvis Presley, becoming in the process one of BMI's most-recorded compositions in the history of popular music. In 1968, "Gentle on My Mind" won John his first two Grammy awards. The song's royalties, which exceeded, on average, $100,000 per year, gave him the financial freedom to explore his other diverse interests.

Eventually, "Gentle on My Mind" also brought John to the attention of musician Tommy Smothers, who was assembling the staff for what was to become the *Smothers Brothers Comedy Hour*. In our WHYY radio interview, John related the story about how Tommy learned about him:

A fellow named Bill Thompson was the music/program director at a station in Los Angeles when "Gentle on My Mind" was way up on the charts. And he was a friend of Jan Howard's of the Grand Ole Opry, who was a good friend of mine. Thompson had gone to school with Tommy Smothers, and he [was the one that] took my record to Tommy Smothers and Mason

Williams. [After hearing my album,] they [then] called me up and flew me to LA.

[Smothers] hired a whole bunch of writers that had never written for television before simply because he wanted new material. He didn't want that same old kind of television stuff. [Writing for the Smothers Brothers] wasn't that much different than writing songs, it was just a matter of being creative. Sometimes we worked in sections around a table where we'd all pitch ideas and a stenographer would take [them] down. And then, other times, we'd all have partners for a week or two. What's interesting is who was on that writers' staff: [comedians and actors] Steve Martin, Rob Reiner, Jerry Music, McLean Stevenson, Bob Einstein, and Carl Gottlieb. Mason Williams [who later had a huge hit with his recording "Classical Gas"] and Allan Blye were the head writers. And everybody brought something different [to the writing room].

Hosted by Tommy and his brother Dick, *The Smothers Brothers Comedy Hour* ran nationally for three seasons from 1967 to 1969 on CBS. The program included sketch comedy featuring a repertoire company of characters interspersed with musical guests. Because of the politically and culturally controversial nature of the series, the Smothers Brothers were constantly locked in a battle with network censors.

Luckily, this was not the case with the eminently more successful and mainstream 1968 summer replacement for Tommy and Dick. Originally titled *The Summer Brothers Smothers Show*, it became *The Glen Campbell Goodtime Hour* when the program joined the regular CBS lineup in 1969. John was initially designated the head writer for Glen, a role he told me that he quickly transcended by starting each week's program with "banjo player stands up in audience, plays 'Gentle on My Mind.'" Of course, that banjo player was John. He was spending more time on the West Coast, and in 1969 left Nashville and his marriage behind.

Even though songwriting and crafting material for television remained John's focus during those years, John kept his identification as a musician. He often quipped that "A banjo will get you through times of no money, but money won't get you times of no banjo." During John's California sojourn, he would spend his weeks rehearsing and taping for television and his weekends performing concerts. Eventually, John assembled a country-rock trio he dubbed Iron Mountain Depot to back him. This was also the name of his last recording RCA issued before John left the label at the end of 1970. Additionally, during John's time on the West Coast, Doubleday published a volume of his poetry and lyrics. Titled *Word Movies*, John promoted the collection with signings throughout 1970 and into 1971. His music publisher Chuck Glaser commented that, from the beginning of their relationship, John had used the phrase to describe his lyrics. "When I write a song," he told Chuck, "I really write a picture. I use the music for emphasis, sort of like a soundtrack behind a movie, or I guess you could say I'm trying to paint with sound."

Also, during the late 1960s and early 1970s, John played on a number of recording sessions for other artists. These included the Byrds (*Sweetheart of the Rodeo*), Delaney and Bonnie (*Motel Shot* and *Together*), James Taylor (*Mud Slide Slim*), James's sibling Kate (*Sister Kate*), Seals and Crofts (*Summer Breeze*), as well as the *Jud* movie soundtrack. Some other albums eventually including John were the Dillards' *Tribute to the American Duck*, Doug Dillard's *You Don't Need a Reason to Sing*, *Tennessee Jubilee* by Benny Martin, *Pickin' in the Wind* from Mark O'Connor, Tom Pacheco's *The Outsider*, Gove Scrivenor's *Shady Gove*, *Dad's Favorites* by Byron Berline, and albums by Vassar Clements, Hoyt Axton, and Guthrie Thomas. John enjoyed helping both aspiring musicians and established performers and would continue this practice for the rest of his life.

> Nobody wrote, sang, or played like him. . . . He can't, rather *won't* change to become something he isn't.
> —JOHNNY CASH, ALBUM NOTES, *JOHN HARTFORD LOOKS AT LIFE*

After the 1969 television season, John left Glen Campbell's program. He made the rounds for the myriad of talk and variety shows on television and was booked onto numerous "specials" hosted by various stars. These appearances continued into the early 1980s.

Additionally, several attempts were made by his management, which he shared with Tommy and Dick Smothers, at creating vehicles that they believed would more completely showcase John's talents. *Just Friends*, an obvious spin-off including the cast of the Smothers Brothers program, was broadcast by ABC. John also hosted *Something Else*, a syndicated musical variety television program sponsored by the American Dairy Association.

Even after John had left Hollywood behind, there were periodic reunions with Tom and Dick Smothers, Glen Campbell, and the various cast members from their programs. Unfortunately, none of these projects provided John with continuing long-term success in mainstream show business (John would later claim he was glad that these attempts never came to fruition).

Some of his lack for securing a place within the conventional entertainment industry resulted from John's discontent with what he thought of as the insincerity of those around him in Hollywood. Later in life, John would often discuss how he had had to relinquish control of his career to achieve mainstream success. Later, he would reclaim this control once his goals were attained (which I assume included access to entertainment resources, along with the resulting recognition, clout, and financial security).

Rather than play the roles on television being offered such as a Columbo-esque detective, John yearned for a return to full-time live performing and music-making. Eventually, he grew tired of the West Coast approach, which attempted to place him in situations (using a riverboat analogy) outside of his wheelhouse. John became less cooperative with his management, growing his hair and beard, and, beginning in 1971, traveling to Nashville to refresh his music.

> Without John Hartford there would be no newgrass.
> —SAM BUSH

After the expiration of his RCA Victor contract in late 1970, John was signed as a solo artist to Warner Bros. Records. He was spending more time back in Tennessee, and John got to jam around Christmas of that year with the duo of Norman Blake and Dobro player and mandolinist Tut Taylor. He had already met guitarist and multi-instrumentalist Blake (born 1938) in 1969 while recording an episode of *The Johnny Cash Show* at the Ryman Auditorium. Norman, a Nashville studio musician, performed and recorded with Johnny before joining the house band for his TV show. Among other notable credits, Norman had backed Bob Dylan on the singer's *Nashville Skyline* LP. Robert Arthur "Tut" Taylor (1923–2015), along with George Gruhn and Randy Wood, was the owner of GTR (for George, Tut, and Randy). Their music store, where Norman also taught stringed instruments, stood several short blocks from the Ryman.

The acoustic, bluegrass-derived music the trio created, along with John's increasing discomfort with Hollywood, inspired him to fire his electrified folk-rock ensemble and replace them by April 1971 with Norman and Tut. With the addition of bluegrass fiddler Vassar Clements, what became known as the Aereo-Plain band was born as John's new group.

When he had begun recording for RCA, John had no choice in the studio but to follow the direction of his producers. John, along with everyone else involved, was looking for hits. Therefore, he went along with the arrangements for studio musicians, strings, and brass generated by industry professionals.

However, by the time of his last two collections for RCA Victor, John had replaced the session "cats" with his road band, Iron Mountain Depot. While the arrangements still leaned mainstream, there was a bit more of a folk-rock feeling added to the resulting sound.

This all went out the window when John joined with Norman, Tut, and Vassar. For his new group, John utilized a more organic approach. When together on the road, he told me, the quartet jammed from the moment they awoke until they went to sleep at night. The four musicians played up until showtime, performed their stage sets, and then "picked" some more afterwards. The music included fiddle tunes and songs from folk and bluegrass traditions, as well as originals generated by all the band members. Some new songs even developed out of ideas attempted during these sessions. These jams and performances were likewise woven in between attempts around recording John's first Warner Bros. album.

John's initial recording for Warner Bros., titled *Aereo-Plain*, featured this quartet. While not a massive seller, it was hugely influential, inspiring the newgrass musical movement, which, like the Aereo-Plain Band, approached bluegrass with a rock 'n' roll attitude.

Interestingly, he had recruited first-time producer David Bromberg for the recording because of, as John stated to me, David's "New York sensibility." After hiring him, John had only two instructions for the nascent supervisor. One, always be rolling tape, even if it's only a two-track rough-mix backup (the album was "officially" recorded on multitrack machines). And, secondly, don't play back anything recorded to the musicians until the finished album was assembled.

It is obvious from the album's outtakes that David played a major role in guiding and shaping that LP's production. In fact, after John believed that the sessions had concluded, Bromberg felt that the results didn't properly focus on John Hartford the songwriter and requested that he compose and record more original material. John told me in that moment, he slammed down the phone in anger and refused to follow David's directive. However, after calming down, he sheepishly called David back and agreed to his suggestion.

So, out went Tut's originals "Ruff and Ready" and "Oasis" and bluegrass standards including "Where the Old Red River Flows," "Dig A Hole [aka "Darling Cory"]," "John Henry," and "Doin' My Time." Additional sessions following Bromberg's suggestion yielded songs such as "Steamboat Whistle Blues," "Up on the Hill Where They Do the Boogie," "Symphony Hall Rag," "Holding," "Because of You," "Tear Down the Grand Ole Opry," and a more fully realized version of "Back in the Goodle Days." Additional record dates at Jimi Hendrix's Electric Lady Studio in New York City produced the two versions of "Turn Your Radio On" that bookend the original LP.

During the same period that *Aereo-Plain* was created, two members of John's band—Norman and Vassar—participated in the Nashville sessions for *Will the Circle Be Unbroken*. Considering that most of his group had been recruited along with close compatriot Earl Scruggs to record with the Nitty Gritty Dirt Band for that project, and that John was a friend and supporter of all those involved, it is puzzling that he wasn't also enlisted for this groundbreaking album.

Sadly, John's revolutionary new ensemble of Vassar Clements, Norman Blake, and Tut Taylor lasted only a year. This was followed by about another twelve months of touring with Norman, during which the recording of John's second Warner Bros. album, *Morning Bugle*, occurred. Throughout this period, the Aereo-Plain band as well as the duo of Hartford and Blake often shared the stage with Earl Scruggs. These interactions resulted in some memorable onstage jamming between John and Earl and strengthened their friendship.

During the phase of his travels between Los Angeles and Nashville in the first part of the 1970s, John wed a second time. His relationship with actress Nawana Davis lasted almost four years, including the short time of their official union (December 26, 1973, through June 1975).

Unfortunately, Warner Bros. never quite figured out how to properly support and market John's music. Their ambivalence in promoting his two albums for the company resulted in John buying his way out of their contract. Around the same time, he switched his booking responsibilities to Keith Case, then based at the Stone County agency in Colorado.

The absence of a subsequent recording agreement began a three-year break from recording for John. With some notable exceptions, it also marked the end of his affiliation with the major labels. From this point forward, John would choose to work with independents or to record for his own imprint.

Trying to describe what it is [that] I love about the river would be like trying to describe what it is I love about my wife.

Away from the studio, John reconnected with the river. In 1973, John began a tradition of spending about ten days during each of the summer months working on the *Julia Belle Swain* out of Peoria, Illinois. John even eventually settled by a body of water, building a Victorian steamboat-inspired home outside of Nashville on the banks of the Cumberland River.

Ultimately, riverboats provided John the impetus to record *Mark Twang*, his first album since leaving Warner Bros. John's debut for Bruce Kaplan's independent Flying Fish Records, this completely solo disc included four original songs about life on the river. "Skippin' in the Mississippi Dew," John's composition recorded for his last (and unreleased at the time) RCA album and recut for *Twang*, was the first published instance of John combining his love of bluegrass music with the river and riverboats. "Long Hot Summer Days," backed by his own fiddling, reflected John's experience working on river craft during his summers back in St. Louis. "Let Him Go On Mama" is a tribute to one of those "old time rivermen" he knew and admired and tried so hard to emulate. And, lastly, "The Julia Belle Swain" described John's life and crewmates on and around that particular steamboat.

John later told Flying Fish's Vice President of Artist Development Seymour Guenther: "We cut [the record] live in two takes, one for each side. I wanted to make it loose and spontaneous, like the radio shows I used to do." Too loose and spontaneous for audio engineer Claude Hill, who insisted that a disclaimer be included on the jacket for the album ("The seemingly technical imperfections in this record which may be indiscernible to the listener, were included at the request of the artist"). But John had the last laugh when *Mark Twang* earned him his third Grammy award.

Steamboating continued as a subject for John's songwriting for the rest of his life. John also included preexisting songs about river travel alongside his own on his recordings and in his performances. This perfectly integrated love of music and affection toward the river led to John's frequent requests to perform on riverboats and at historical river events. He became the first-call entertainer for any affair remotely connected to boats and waterways.

One of his personal high points came in 1987, when John was officially licensed to pilot steamboats. Near the end of his life, John was heartbroken when the illness that would eventually claim his life forced him to forfeit that pilot's certificate.

John later reflected that the river "becomes a metaphor for a whole lot of things, and I find for some mysterious reason that if I stay in touch with it things seem to work out all right." As John told Marty Moss-Cohane, the host of WHYY's *Radio Times*, "Trying to describe what it is [that] I love about the river would be like trying to describe what it is I love about my wife."

Hartford himself is getting more and more warped with every appearance here; his old "Gentle on My Mind" identity has now been quite handily replaced by a Hartford whose true art lies in mixing fine music with calmly bizarre lyrics and making it work.

—JEANI REED, *PROVINCE*

From the fall of 1972 when Norman Blake embarked on his own career as a front man through the 1976 release of *Mark Twang*, John had to learn how to command a large audience as a solo performer. Appearing alone made economic sense, as did the relative simplicity of traveling on one's own. Initially flying from gig to gig, John eventually followed in the footsteps of his country music forebears by purchasing a bus. He hired several drivers who could also handle sound mixing and brought along his third wife to sell product such as records and T-shirts.

As John remarked, when he started out on RCA, he would just sit onstage and sing his introspective songs. Live recordings and reviews reinforce that between 1967 and 1973, John did not have much of an "act" outside of playing his music. Luckily, this was soon to be changed by this resourceful, always experimenting musician.

At the end of the Aereo-Plain band's tenure, John had laid the groundwork for a solo style when he began experimenting with lower-pitched banjos "to match my voice." A combination of historical connection and the search for sustain on an instrument normally lacking that characteristic led John to low-tuned banjos. Their relaxed timbre helped to fill the musical space in a solo situation.

However, more was required to make up for his lack of a musical group. Initially, John experimented with a drum machine for his backup. He eventually hit upon the idea of accompanying himself by step dancing in time to his music. John traced the origin of his onstage movements to Norman Blake. After viewing John's performance antics, Blake commented that all John additionally needed to include was dancing. Then, Norman sardonically added, he would really have something.

Luckily for John, his appearances at folk and bluegrass festivals brought him into contact with modern country dance groups such as the Green Grass Cloggers. Their performance version of American clogging appeared alongside John at summer music events. It was executed using the figures from traditional square and line dancing. These ensembles consisted of the male/female couples utilized in the informal rural house dances from days of yore. Some of the dancers ingeniously invented small, portable one-person wooden stepping platforms that could be brought to campground jam sessions. Both the "step-a-tunes," as they were dubbed, as well as these movements were witnessed, interpreted, and integrated by John into his solo performances.

For a period before he acquired his first bus, flying necessitated requiring events to provide an "A grade, 4' x 8' x ¾" plywood" sheet for his stepping. John eventually rigged his "dancing board" with a pickup run through a phase shifter. This led to one bit of stage business where John "tuned" this panel to his fiddle by tapping on the plywood platform with his bow.

John's final solo supplement was the electrification of his acoustic guitar, fiddle, and banjo. By "plugging in" with pickups, John was able to be louder than with just microphones. He also employed a wireless setup that freed him to wander about the stage and even into the audience if he so desired, adding another visual element to his performances.

John began adding other ways for keeping the attention of a large festival audience with just his voice, his instruments, and his feet. One was by turning each set into several long medleys rather than taking traditional breaks between selections. Utilizing many tempo and key changes, John would weave his own compositions, bluegrass chestnuts, and instrumental pieces together before switching to a different instrument.

Another method employed was to eliminate talking from his appearances. Tommy Smothers exposed John to old-time vaudevillians such as George Carl, who executed his comedic bits without speaking. Inspired by performers like Carl, John began eschewing spoken song introductions.

When John did speak, he was likely to tell a prepared fable that reflected his off-kilter sense of the absurd. Taking television's yule log broadcasts past their logical conclusion, one story involved a TV channel which only programmed a fireplace:

My life's ambition is to someday have my own television station. I'd have one studio with a big fireplace in it and a camera focused on the fireplace. And that's what I'd show twenty-four hours a day, seven days a week. It'd just be this fire, see. And, if you got bored with watching what's on the other channels, why, you could just tune in the fire. Get it all focused in there in color, get the sound just right, pull up a rocking chair on each side of the television set, and play checkers. And I'm gonna encourage people to hang rifles over their television sets. For advertising, I'm gonna get a stack of shirt cardboards and some magic markers and write the name of the sponsor on the shirt cardboard and just throw it in the fire.

John also played to his audience through a heavy use of "stoned" humor in his lyrics and the subject matter of his songs. John embraced the drug culture of the times, becoming a consumer of marijuana and writing many songs about it. One reviewer called him "the Will Rogers of the let's-get-stoned-and-play-bluegrass world" (*Kansas City Star*). At the very least, John reflected a popular counterculture sensibility back to his audience.

The last "trick" used by John was to, figuratively, make the audience members a part of his band, therefore engaging his listeners in a total participatory experience. This was accomplished through getting those assembled to clap along and "repeat after me" short lyrical phrases or sounds. In the ultimate inclusion of those gathered, John often closed his sets by "calling" a large square dance that often went on for thirty-plus minutes. As Michael Quinlan wrote in the *Louisville Courier-Journal*, "Audience participation is an integral part of Hartford's show."

Although fans responded favorably to John's stage antics, it took a while for the media covering him to become accustomed to his new solo show. A writer for the *Manhattan* (Kansas) *Mercury* criticized a mid-1970s concert thusly:

Hartford relied heavily on novelty and sophomoric humor in his act; his approach was almost vaudevillian, though more properly it should be described as burlesque. His lyrics . . . were often arch little jokes and japes, sometimes witty, sometimes tedious, a mélange of the risqué and the risible.

Coupled to this was his vocal delivery which verged on the expressive capabilities of Gerald McGoing Boing [*sic; Gerald*

McBoing Boing was a 1950 animated Oscar-winning short featuring a boy who speaks through sound effects], filled with
groans, pants, and intimation of tumescence [readiness for
sexual activity] or tenesmus [bowel evacuation], all from the
impressionist's panoply of sound effects and odd noises. The
novelty of it was quite entertaining initially, but the clever noises
began to wear a bit thin after a while. (Steve Coulson, *Manhattan Mercury*)

Interestingly, in the same year John recorded *Mark Twang*, he also
invited an all-star band into the studio to make what was released
as its follow-up, *Nobody Knows What You Do*. Those albums were
succeeded by two collaborations with his longtime musical buddies
Douglas and Rodney Dillard (1977, 1980), *All in the Name of Love*
(1977), *Headin' Down into the Mystery Below* (1978), *Slumberin' on the
Cumberland* (with Pat Burton and Benny Martin, 1979), *You and Me
at Home* (1980), a solo reworking of selections from his RCA recordings titled *Catalogue* (1981), and *Vassar Clements-John Hartford-Dave
Holland* (Rounder Records, 1984; all others for Flying Fish Records).
   Across these releases were a mix of John's compositions with traditional songs and tunes reflecting his continued interest in riverboats,
Victorian America, and bluegrass music. On those where John didn't
share the spotlight with his current material, he covered his own creations from his old, at the time out-of-print RCA and Warner Bros.
albums. When not performing alone, his LPs featured a "country-rock"
backing including drums and electric and steel guitars. John's new
songs from this phase, with a few notable exceptions, were forget-
table and, therefore, not surprisingly, never found a permanent spot
in his live shows.
   One notable recorded exception during this ten-year period was
Headin' Down into the Mystery Below, another collection of originals
about boats and the river that included John's homage to fourth-
grade teacher Ruth Ferris. John sounds present and engaged. For my
money, it is one of John's best recordings, matching or possibly even
surpassing *Mark Twang*.

You spend the second half of your life
apologizing for the first.

At the end of 1980, John was diagnosed with neck cancer. About six weeks of appearances were cancelled while John had surgery in St. Louis. He probably returned to his childhood home to be under the supervision of his physician father and with care as he recovered from his doting mother. He was to survive that first brush with the disease. However, cancer was to shadow John for the rest of his truncated life.

This diagnosis and his subsequent recuperation prompted John's marriage to his third wife, the former Susan Marie Fielder Barrett (born 1934). John had met Barrett about 1970 at Glaser Brothers publishing, where Marie worked at the time. After the nuptials, John permanently moved from Los Angeles back to Nashville.

Just as John was recovering from his illness, his mother, Mary, died as a result of an automobile accident. Dr. Harford had been the driver and John blamed the premature death of his mother, with whom he was still extremely close, on his father. Following Mary's passing in February 1981, Carl Harford would remarry. Dr. Harford died on May 18, 1992.

The cancer proved a wake-up call for John, who used the onset of the disease as a time for reflection and reassessment. One example of John's personal growth and rebirth following his initial diagnosis occurred in November 1989. That month, fellow musician and television host David Holt lost his ten-year-old daughter, Sara Jane, in a motor vehicle collision. John had performed several times on Holt's TNN (The Nashville Network) cable television program *Fire on the Mountain*, and the two had appeared at the same musical events since at least 1975. Upon hearing of Sara Jane's passing, John appeared at the Holt home outside of Asheville, North Carolina, and stayed at David's side throughout his daughter's funeral. David Holt comments that John kept in the background the whole time and never behaved like John Hartford the star but as a friend.

John's influence was further felt by Holt when he encouraged David's return to performing. Within two weeks of the death of his eldest child, David was scheduled to appear in Salisbury, North Carolina. Fearing he wouldn't be in any emotional condition to entertain,

David was prepared to cancel the engagement. John talked David into going, telling him, "If you don't get back on the horse now, you'll never do it. You were put on this earth to play music and the best way to honor your daughter's memory is to continue to perform." I believe that John was drawing upon his own recent experiences, repeating his own advice to himself following the passing of his mother under similar circumstances. David got musician Laura Boosinger to accompany him for the concert and somehow got through the evening.

Rather than interpret his cancer as a death sentence, John was to view his survival as an opportunity. Determined to live life to the fullest and to reform some of his past behaviors, John saw new possibilities and a second chance at living. John emerged from his initial cancer treatments as a kinder, more empathetic individual. He shed the ego he had developed in Hollywood and became more interested in other people. As John would often say, "You spend the second half of your life apologizing for the first." I believe without this transformation, John and I would have never become friends and musical collaborators.

CHAPTER TWO

THE MASTER OF HIGH LACONIC

Let's all go to the old back room, and pray for no blue food
Bull Durham and the second coming, at the altar of pinto beans
Put the best of the worst on first my dear, and the worst of the best
*   on last*
The inebriated church of the latter day drunk, for sheep as opposed
*   to goat gut string*
Low bass tone bust your gall stone buddy, from the tune of the
*   very same name*
—"MORE BIG BULL FIDDLE FUN"

Hartford has established himself as the master of High Laconic [*sic*].
—JOHN T. DAVIS, *AUSTIN AMERICAN-STATESMAN*

After successfully beating back cancer in 1981, John settled into a comfortable existence. He performed between forty and a hundred dates per year, although for most, John limited appearances to about fifty to sixty throughout the United States and Canada. In the winter, he plied the club circuit. John spent his summers at festivals such as Telluride, Newport Folk Festival, Chicago Folk Festival, Philadelphia Folk Festival, Joe Val Memorial Festival, MerleFest, and the Strawberry Festival. For one recurring gig, John would decamp every October for the Fall Homecoming at the Museum of Appalachia in East Tennessee. There, he would appear daily on stage between long periods in jam sessions.

John also found time for performances on television, including David Letterman's late-night show, *American Music Shop*, and *The Smothers Brothers Comedy Hour: 20th Reunion*, and radio, on programs such as *Nashville Now, Lonesome Pine Special, Liberty Flyer, A Prairie Home Companion, Grand Ole Opry*, and *Mountain Stage*. John became a particular favorite on TNN (The Nashville Network), a cable channel based in Nashville featuring country performers.

He additionally appeared at tribute concerts benefiting a variety of causes, preferring to lend his talents to assist musicians, musical organizations, and river-oriented groups. Since John was a longtime lover of bluegrass music, when the International Bluegrass Music Association (IBMA) was formed in 1985, he was an early participant. He initially hosted the IBMA awards show and played an integral part in that organization's Fan Fest.

And, in his spare time, John piloted the *Julia Belle Swain*.

He had successfully transitioned from sensitive singer-songwriter in the mid-1960s to late-1960s folk-rocker to newgrass band leader in the early 1970s, and, for the remainder of the 1970s, an electrified wide-eyed hippie prankster. Finally, for his middle age during the 1980s, John distanced himself from these prior images to become a Victorian riverboat pilot. This shift was reflected in his onstage clothing and a growing discomfort with performing some of his most extreme drug-themed original material.

For this mature persona, John shed T-shirts and jeans for more emblematic clothing. About 1980, he began wearing a derby onstage. By the following year, he had added two or three vests to his garb. John's numerous vests, while enhancing his appearance, also served as a mobile file cabinet. Their multiple pockets housed 3-by-5-inch cards (I once witnessed him contritely correct a fan who referred to them as "4-by-5") containing the analog version of a modern-day mobile phone. The file cards contained John's address book, calendar, and song ideas, along with various bits and pieces of information that were feeding his curiosity. He separated the cards into various categories, with each held together with a rubber band wrapped diagonally around two opposing corners. The third component of his stage costume were spectator or wingtip footwear. To complement this image,

John developed a flowing cursive handwriting, which he utilized on album covers and to inscribe those jackets for adoring fans.

What became John's trademark hat, shoes, and waistcoats evoked everyone from early country music star Uncle Dave Macon to nineteenth-century traveling salesmen, train conductors, and sideshow barkers. John created the impression of tradition through a nostalgic representation for things past—riverboats, square dances, and rural life. John, the Victorian gentleman, had emerged.

The "derby and vest" John is the one that joined me for our radio interview in the summer of 1985. For our time together that day, between sampling four of his recordings, I focused on questions about his early life and career leading up to his move to Los Angeles to write for the Smothers Brothers television program. The biggest takeaway from this initial face-to-face was the connection we made on a personal level. Although he had told these stories many times before our interaction, I was impressed by John's enthusiasm, openness, and appreciation for my own banjo playing.

NOW LET'S HAVE A BIG HAND FOR ABSOLUTELY NO REASON WHATSOEVER.

Along with his new image, John's performances evolved as well. By the late 1980s, he had unplugged and begun to offer audiences spoken interludes between his musical selections in the style of a slightly off-kilter vaudevillian. A student of language, these vignettes were a combination of old-time rural expressions such as "tickled to death" and "reared back" and the urban jargon found in the writings of Ogden Nash and other scribblers located within the pages of the *New Yorker*, which John faithfully read throughout his entire life. Some of these were routines with punchlines, some were one-liners, and still others were more in the form of philosophical musings. Some of my favorite examples:

A little old man comes home and tells his wife, "Honey, you'll never guess what I did today. I went out and bought us a condominium." She replied, "Great, I can stop using my diagram."

A young lady come [*sic*] up to me about twenty-five years ago and she looked me right square in the eye, she said, "I wish you'd sing something I know so I could tell if you were any good or not."

Flattery will get you everywhere.

It's just as well that this music will never become any more popular than it already is. Because if it ever does, we're just going to have to share it with a whole lot of people that we don't know or even like. Right now, not only do we all know each other but there's a chance that a good many of us are related.

A fellow goes to the doctor. He has a carrot sticking out of his nose, a turnip in his ear, and a zucchini in his ass. He asks the doctor what's wrong with him and the doctor says, "Well, for one thing, you're not eating right."

You all are wonderful. You did that [sang along] like you all came in the same car together and everybody rode in the back seat.

We're mighty proud that you're here, I'm mighty proud that I'm here, and I'm especially proud that we're all here at the same time.

My wife, Marie, said that fiddle tunes all sounded alike and had funny names. And I said, that's what I liked about them.

A guy jumps out of an airplane and, about halfway down, his parachute won't open. He sees someone coming up at him and, as he passes, he asks, "Do you know anything about parachutes?" The other fellow says, "I sure don't. Do you know anything about Coleman stoves?"

One of John's longer stories concerned being invited to a party. His host's long-winded explanation about everything that was planned for that evening's celebration got more and more debauched as it went along. When John finally asked what time the festivities began, his friend replied that it didn't matter, because "there won't be anybody [there] but you and me."

"I'M STILL HERE"

It was during the 1980s that John began to develop his "formula" for making albums. As he explained it to me, each collection would include new compositions alongside remakes of some of his older songs currently unavailable on disc, and a few traditional pieces and classics by other performers. John was to (loosely) follow this concept for the rest of his life.

In 1984, John began a musical alliance with Jack Clement and Jack's disciple Mark Howard. This relationship resulted in a series of three recordings, the first titled *Gum Tree Canoe*. Produced by Clement, *Gum Tree* featured the return by John to a more mainstream recording style closer to what was found on his RCA albums.

Along with the arrangements, his new original songs were quite different from those on all of John's prior LPs. He began utilizing fewer words to communicate his sentiments. Within the lush arrangements, John's lyrical choices became simpler, more direct, and more romantic. Even his love songs contained a nostalgia that his earlier compositions, representing the times in which they were composed, did not.

As I wrote in the notes for the 2001 CD reissue of *Gum Tree Canoe*:

> In the early 1980s, John [re]recorded his song "I'm Still Here [originally on 1968's *Housing Project*]." In part, Hartford was signaling that, although the music business had gone through several changes during his involvement, he was still performing and recording. John was also alerting his audience to the fact that the *Gum Tree Canoe* LP marked a change in his approach to making records. Gone were "live in the studio" minimalist outings such as *Mark Twang*, *Headin' Down into the Mystery Below* and *Catalogue*, and the studio supersessions of *All in the Name of Love* and *Slumberin' on the Cumberland*. With the addition of Jack Clement, whom John had known

since his days at RCA Records (and, later, Clement's protégé, Mark Howard) as producer, Hartford embarked on a series of highly polished studio productions. Clement's philosophy, as John tells it, was to massage the original recordings, adding and subtracting from the basic tracks, until the pieces flowed invisibly before the listeners' ears.

As Jack Clement spent more and more time creating the final mixes, the budget for *Gum Tree* headed for the stratosphere. Up until this time, John had funded (and therefore owned) the masters for all his Flying Fish albums. Because John and his wife were loath to lay out so much cash toward Jack's spending, John traded the rights for his prior records to Flying Fish in exchange for the label covering all of Jack Clement's expenses (he had already assigned Jack his publishing rights to get the producer onto the project). Because Jack Clement's "massage" of the recordings went on so long, John had to drive to Jack's home studio and physically wrestle the reels of tape away from him in order to release the album.

The *Gum Tree Canoe* sessions included John's original recordings for many songs that were destined to become staples of his live show for years to come. These included (interestingly enough) three that were written by others: the Civil War anthem "Lorena," Victorian heart song "Gum Tree Canoe," and the Flatt & Scruggs mainstay, "I Wonder Where You Are Tonight."

One of the most interesting ways *Gum Tree* was promoted was through the nascent form of the music video. In an archetypically John move, he decided to save money with a shoot utilizing one home video camera. The song he chose to highlight was a cover of the soul standard "Little Piece of My Heart," most recently popularized in 1968 by Janis Joplin (under the correct title of "Piece of My Heart"). For the clip, among other short shots detailing his facial features and feet, John employed one of his offbeat ideas by mostly showing his fingers moving on the banjo. As he often explained, John saw the close-ups of hand movements as the equivalent of filming figures dancing.

Gum Tree Canoe was the first of John's renewed attempts toward the goal of reaching a wider audience. He wanted his records played once again on commercial radio, and for his bookings to increase in number, price, and quality. At the very least, the trio of Hartford, Clement, and Howard were aiming for a major-label contract. This goal was achieved when John signed what became a one-album deal with MCA/Dot Records in the fall of 1986. The resulting platter, titled *Annual Waltz* after one of John's original songs, was released in January 1987.

To adequately represent *Gum Tree Canoe* and, later, *Annual Waltz*, on stage, John assembled the first Hartford Stringband. For initial performances, he recruited fiddler Jonathan Yudkin, guitarist Mark Howard, and bassist Roy Huskey Jr. from the recording sessions, naming them the Derby String Band.

By September 1987, with the addition of fiddlers Ruth McGuiness and Holly Odell, the group officially became the Hartford Stringband. Yudkin, McGuiness, and Odell were classically trained fiddlers active in teaching, in Nashville studios, as well as in country and bluegrass backing bands. Huskey was a first-call Nashville bassist whose father had played bass on countless hit country records in the 1960s. This ensemble existed through early 1990, recording on John's next album, *Down on the River* (Flying Fish Records, 1989). That collection included some of his most enduring songs, comprising, besides the title cut, "Here I Am in Love Again" and "Delta Queen Waltz," named for the steamboat. The Stringband performed with John at Nashville venues as well as the IBMA's annual Fan Fest.

Annual Waltz, which pictures John dancing with his wife, Marie, on the cover, and *Down on the River* included his most direct and nostalgic love songs to date. The lush string arrangements and recordings polished to a high sheen only serve to reinforce the sensibilities of these compositions.

John credits his son, Jamie, for teaching him to read music at the beginning of the 1980s. This allowed John to visualize his musical concepts on paper for the first time. Additionally, it enabled him to communicate these melodies directly to other players.

The dense violin-centric arrangements of that initial Stringband were, I believe, a collaboration between John, who provided the ideas, with Yudkin, who understood the rules of harmony and had the classical chops to commit complex compositions to paper. Somewhat humorously, I would describe the results as Beethoven writing for bluegrass father Bill Monroe, who also (for a period) had employed multiple fiddlers. At the very least, it was John and Jack Clement paying tribute to Owen Bradley, Billy Sherrill, and the Nashville Sound: a bit staid, but nonetheless what John was after for these recordings.

During this same period, John also found time to produce and record two albums for West Virginia banjoist Elmer Bird, *Bumble Bee Waltz* (1985) and *Turkey Creek* (1987). John fiddled along with Bird's straight-ahead down-picking style for a mixture of traditional and new tunes by Elmer. John also authored the picture book *Steamboat in a Cornfield*. Released in the year between Bird's recordings, John had originally taken the true story of a boat run aground and repurposed it into a song lyric. However, when the result proved too long to sing, John converted the prose, with the addition of historical photographs, into a children's book.

Additionally, 1986 saw the release of John's collaboration with the Deering Banjo Company. The John Hartford model banjo was a continuation of experiments into "finding a banjo that matched my voice" that John had begun in 1972. After initially repurposing preexisting vintage banjos for low tunings, in 1982 he commissioned Stelling Banjo to build him an instrument with a wooden tone ring. Their collaboration continued the following year, with the debut of his own model (which they continued making for ten years).

John and Deering produced various versions of a Hartford model. They utilized different scale lengths and number of frets, and inlay designed by John influenced by the type of Victorian filigreed decorations found on steamboats. A version of this low-pitched instrument is still being manufactured today by Deering and has been utilized by musicians such as Bela Fleck and Alison Brown.

THERE WON'T BE ANYBODY BUT YOU AND ME.

I visited John's home for the first time during the winter of 1986. After conducting a banjo workshop at Cedars of Lebanon State Park east of Nashville, Calvin Minner (later one of the organizers for the Tennessee Banjo Institute and an employee of Gruhn Guitars, the successor to GTR) brought me to Madison, north of Nashville proper. The occasion coincided with the day luthier Scott Didlake was delivering a gourd banjo he had made for John.

The original cabin on the Hartford property had been what John labeled a "fish camp": a cottage with basic amenities utilized in the summer months or on weekends as a getaway from the city. One drove north from the East Nashville neighborhood up Gallatin Road to Madison, along a route passing to the west of the cemetery where country musicians Roy Acuff, Jimmy Martin, and now John and Marie Hartford are buried. Turning east toward the Cumberland River, one traversed a long gravel drive to reach his house perched atop the riverbank. One entered the structure across a narrow porch into an open box including an L-shaped living/dining space with a fireplace and windows on three sides (John always said it reminded him of being on a steamboat, which is probably what attracted him to the building in the first place). John's old office sat under the cottage through a trapdoor. An attic was used for storage. The galley kitchen was reached by walking straight past the fireplace along the rear of the home.

By the occasion for my first visit, an addition had been made to the section farthest from the river. Turning left after entering the front door, one passed John's library on the way into his second office, next to which was a bath and, behind the kitchen, a television viewing room with large closets. During our friendship, further appendages were made, with the Hartfords eventually adding an entire open-floor concept Victorian home onto the rear of the original cabin. John's office gained a second room, with three floors of additional living and office space, including bedrooms, bathrooms, screened porches, and a cupola with river views. It was a great home for John and Marie. However, I was uncomfortable staying there, as the large open rooms lacked privacy and put you in everyone's way.

I don't remember much about that initial visit except for some good fellowship and John's hospitality. I was probably a bit in awe of being at Hartford's home. As most of the day was taken up with Scott showing off his newly constructed instrument to John, nothing much else probably happened. As I would become a frequent visitor to the Hartford residence after 1991, the many occasions spent on the banks of the Cumberland River tend to run together into one overlapping memory.

Following that occasion, I began attending John's performances as his guest. Initially, I would see John's concerts as a member of the audience. However, by the middle of 1988, John began to invite me up during his shows to participate in the occasional selection. From that time through 1990, as both John and I kept busy schedules, this only amounted to a few appearances per year. However, all was to change the following year, when I began my participation with John on a series of recorded projects.

The Fun of Open Discussion

Our switch from friendship into collaboration occurred at the beginning of 1991. Without my noticing, John and I began work on what would eventually become the second of our two duet projects. In retrospect, I'm aware that John probably made a conscious decision to involve me on some level in his music. At the very least, he was just, as he so often put it, doing "what's in my heart because if nobody likes it, at least I haven't wasted my time."

John once told me that, when he had started out learning music in Missouri, he always wanted to play the fiddle in jam sessions and with the bands of which he was a member. However, everyone else preferred him to concentrate on the banjo. Therefore, for many years, although retaining his chops on the former, he focused and became identified with the latter. It was only after John became obsessed with Ed Haley (about whom more later) did he redirect his musical interests toward the violin.

I believe that one reason John chose me as an accomplice once he began to follow his fiddle fanaticism is that he saw someone who understood what he would label the "language" of traditional fiddling. He often drew upon one of his sayings when telling those assembled, "This boy doesn't play the fiddle, but he knows when one is being played."

As our friendship deepened, what became apparent was that John's stage show didn't adequately reflect his true musical interests. (This isn't unusual for many of the commercially successful people I've known.) John's somewhat gimmicky and glib onstage persona only

Bob Carlin and John Hartford: The Fun of Open Discussion (CD cover, Rounder Records, 1995). Cover art by James Alan Higgins, design by Nancy Given. At the beginning of 1991, my relationship with John transitioned from friendship to collaboration. We began work on what would become the second of our duet projects, The Fun of Open Discussion.

hinted at the depth and range of his tastes and pursuits. Only during offstage jam sessions or in private conversations would the scope of John's knowledge for bluegrass standards and traditional fiddle tunes reveal itself. My witnessing the offstage John Hartford effected the final change in my opinion toward John's onstage music.

In January 1991, John stopped by my home in North Carolina. He was in the midst of a major tour with the Glen Campbell Goodtime Hour Revisited, with whom he would make half of his documented appearances that year. I hosted a jam session that included Dale O'Bryant and myself on banjos (Dale was cousin of the Nashville

Bluegrass Band's Alan O'Bryant and taught with me at Davidson County Community College, now Davidson-Davie Community College). For half of the session, John fiddled bluegrass standards to include Dale in the proceedings. For the other half he played some of his current favorite tunes that would become the basis for the first Hartford/Carlin album, *The Fun of Open Discussion*. In retrospect, John was obviously testing the waters for a possible fiddle/banjo recording with me.

That spring, John called regarding a different project. Bruce Nemerov and Paul Wells of the Center for Popular Music at Middle Tennessee State University had approached John about participating on one of their recordings. Time-Life had contracted MTSU to produce a boxed set titled *The Civil War Music Collector's Edition*. For his part of the proceedings, John wanted my expertise on minstrel-period banjo.

Therefore, about the end of May or early June 1991, I headed for Nashville. Upon my arrival, John, fiddler Frazier Moss, and I spent a day at Mark O'Connor's fiddle camp, rehearsed for our recording sessions, played the Grand Ole Opry, and made our first attempts at recording the *Fun* album at John's abode. (Mark had first come to Nashville in 1976 as a wunderkind to make a solo record that featured John, and Mark had returned the favor by appearing with John on *Gum Tree Canoe*. O'Connor always welcomed him and whichever musicians he had in tow to his camps as a guest performer.)

On June 3 and 4, John and I entered Mark Howard's recording studio. As the John Hartford–named Bob 'n' John Minstrels (our logo, as drawn by John, featured a fiddle and banjo floating in a toilet), we waxed "Jordan Is a Hard Road to Travel," "I Wish I Was in Dixie's Land" and an unreleased parody of "Jordan," "Richmond Is a Hard Road to Travel." I cut a solo performance of "Old Dan Tucker" and John recorded two versions of "Lorena," which he had previously included on *Gum Tree Canoe*.

John first performed "Lorena" as a barbershop quartet, overdubbing all the vocal parts in a mock voice à la the 1960s animated cartoon character Dudley Do-Right. As somewhat expected, when project producer Paul Wells was presented with the results, he insisted that John redo the song in a more conventional solo vocal and guitar version. This resulted in a confrontation between Hartford and Wells.

John tended to test people by pushing at their boundaries, and this session was no exception. I was to discover that John, utilizing a technique he had learned in childhood when a situation wasn't going his way, would show anger and sometimes storm out (such as his interaction with David Bromberg during the recording of *Aereo-Plain*). Since that time recording *The Civil War Music Collector's Edition*, I witnessed a few other occasions where John employed this practice to achieve his goals (as during the *True Life Blues* project discussed later in this chapter). Usually, John felt that he had nothing to lose, as he believed those involved needed him more than he needed them, so he got his way.

However, on this occasion, Paul Wells stood his ground, and John was persuaded to rerecord the song. That remake was included in the subsequent CD release. This and the other performances were issued on October 17, 1991, by Time-Life.

By the following year, John had completed thirteen albums for the Flying Fish label. With the unexpected passing of label founder Bruce Kaplan at year's end, John's association with that company concluded. In place of Flying Fish, John and Marie chose to start their own record imprint. They titled the company Small Dog A-Barkin' after Marie's dog Bus, who is pictured on their discs in a possibly unwitting reference to Nipper, the emissary for RCA Victor.

The Hartfords began CD releases with *Goin' Back to Dixie*, a standard set of John Hartford originals and traditional material, as well as the all-instrumental *Cadillac Rag*. The former debuted the original river song "M.I.S.I.P." and included John's tribute to Earl Scruggs, "The Boys from North Carolina." The latter collection of John's original tunes had begun life as a 1990 surprise birthday present from John's engineer, producer, and sometimes bandmate Mark Howard. Recorded without John's knowledge at Jack Clement's studio, it included Jonathan Yudkin fiddling Hartford's pieces accompanied by Howard on guitar and mandolin along with Roy Huskey on bass. After John heard the results, Mark was persuaded to add John's banjo to the proceedings and the tracks were ready for commercial release. Or, I should say, *non*-commercial release. While John's Small Dog discs that mixed arrangements of traditional songs with his own compositions sold well, instrumental collections such as *Cadillac Rag* and John's duet CD with Texas Shorty (see below) weren't as popular. Which is a shame, because both *Cadillac Rag* and the Shorty/Hartford *Old Sport* are worth owning. By 2001, Small Dog had produced a half-dozen releases.

During two 1992 shows, I joined John and his son, Jamie, onstage for a few fiddle tunes. John had left his first wife, Jamie's mother Betty, soon after the birth of Jamie's younger sister, Katie. Jamie and Katie were raised by Betty and her second husband. Therefore, Jamie Harford saw little of his biological father after the age of around four or five, until he was a teen in the 1980s. Katie, although raised in the Nashville area, had no real relationship with her birth father until her first child (John's granddaughter) was born at the end of 1996.

Jamie Harford (sometimes spelled "Hartford" like his father) first showed musical ability and ambition as a teenager. He began writing songs and honing his craft by playing on sessions and in Nashville clubs. Jamie started working with his dad on mandolin and vocals in December 1988, consistently accompanying John throughout 1989 and 1990. Their collaboration culminated with the CD titled *Hartford & Hartford*, released by Flying Fish in 1991 (John's last album of new recordings for the label). Thereafter, Jamie Harford was devoted to his own career, but still appeared at scattered concerts and on occasional recordings alongside his father.

With the departure of Jamie Harford, John began searching for a mandolinist/vocalist to continue their duo sound. Jamie's replacement materialized at the October 1992 Tennessee Fall Homecoming. Held at the Museum of Appalachia in Norris, the facility and festival were the creation of John Rice Irwin, an extravagant promoter for local history through his collection of artifacts. Irwin also "collected" individuals he deemed interesting, including musicians such as John Hartford, writers like *Roots* author Alex Haley, as well as regional reenactors of historic crafts and foodways.

John had become a Homecoming fixture at least as early as 1985 (the annual event had debuted in 1979). The format of the festival, with its short stage sets and long offstage jam sessions, allowed John to experiment with different combinations of musicians. On any particular day, as John would often bring his jam partners onstage for his appearances, one never knew whom his band would include.

At the 1992 event, John was reintroduced to Michael Curtis Compton. Born in Meridian, Mississippi, in 1956, Mike's move to Nashville in the late 1970s placed him at the center of bluegrass music. By the middle of the 1980s, he had helped found the Nashville Bluegrass Band, where he was part of their vocal quartet and showcased his expertise in the mandolin stylings of Bill Monroe. After a serious tour bus accident in 1988, Mike spent a year away from Nashville and music. When Compton became reacquainted with John, he was recording and performing with guitarist David Grier. Mike's initial run with Grier, interspersed with occasional John Hartford performances, lasted until the end of 1994. After a break from John in 1995, Mike rejoined full-time. For the next two years, Mike Compton performed with John alongside various bass players. In 1998, when John formed his second Stringband, Compton continued on mandolin until the end of John's life.

Since John was born between the Christmas and New Year's holidays, he began a tradition of hosting a large, multiday celebration at year's end. Starting sometime in the 1980s, Marie would put out a table-groaner of a buffet and the Hartford home would fill with musicians both famous and anonymous. These birthday/Christmas gatherings ended in the early 1990s, and my wife, Rachel, and I attended two of the last ones.

Rachel has been a lifelong (mostly amateur) musician and is well acquainted with bluegrass and country music. However, since she had never met or seen many stars up close, she was blissfully ignorant of the specific ones surrounding her at the Hartford abode. One night, Rachel was seated between two songwriters on a couch in John and Marie's front room. The man on her left turned out to be Harlan Howard, the cowriter of many country hits, including, most famously, "I Fall to Pieces," a smash for Patsy Cline, and "Pick Me Up on My Way Down." At another point in the party, she asked me who were the two men playing guitar and mandolin. I informed her, "That's Benny Martin and Bill Monroe." Bill was crowned the Father of Bluegrass Music by Ralph Rinzler of the Newport Folk Festival and Benny had fiddled for both Monroe and Flatt & Scruggs, as well as having his own solo career. Both were good friends of John's. Rachel also remembers how it was someone's job to stand by the home's front entrance and fetch John when new celebrities arrived.

As one might expect, there were constant jam sessions filling the many rooms, with John the center of attention the whole time. One year, when I was trying to play old-time fiddle tunes with Brad Leftwich (Brad played on my 1985 album for Rounder, *Banging and Sawing*), we were chased from room to room by a group of Texas-style musicians. They kept crashing our session and hijacking it into contest tunes before driving us away. By the third or fourth time this happened, Brad and I had progressed from the first floor to a screened porch at the top level of the house. We finally had to give up playing when even the unheated gallery lacked sanctuary from these "jam-busters."

In September 1992, Earl and Louise Scruggs's son Steve and his family had passed away. When this happened, John canceled his fall appearance at the International Bluegrass Music Association awards show to be with Earl. So, when the couple appeared at John's that December, they were still obviously in shock over the premature deaths of their son, daughter-in-law, and grandchildren.

I was standing with John when Earl and Louise arrived. Upon inquiring how they were doing, Earl indicated how much understandable emotional pain they were in. John and I shouldn't have been so surprised by the Scruggs's appearance, as Earl and Louise really valued their friendship with him. In the coming year, when Earl Scruggs was on the verge of quitting music, John was often at Earl's home, offering words of encouragement to the older man (ironically, he outlived John by over ten years).

The year 1994 was the busiest in the history of Small Dog A-Barkin', with the label releasing three CDs. The first was *Old Sport*. Recorded in John's first office in the basement under the original part of his home, it documented a jam with Texas-style fiddle protégé James David "Texas Shorty" Chancellor. Born in 1943, Texas Shorty had been playing music in his home state from the age of seven. Once Shorty began fiddling and competing as a teenager, he took the premier prize in most of contests he entered. His first "World Championship" was attained in Crockett, Texas, in 1959, where Shorty was the youngest fiddler to win first place. He was to take the honor twice more. Eventually, Shorty achieved one of our nation's highest prizes given for the traditional arts: in 2010, he was awarded a National Endowment for the Arts Heritage Fellowship.

John had initially heard about Shorty in St. Louis from fiddler Cleo Persinger (1909–1971; John sometimes misspelled Cleo's last name "Pursinger"). The founder of the Missouri Fiddlers' Association, Persinger, who farmed outside Columbia, Missouri, several hours west of St. Louis, was active at state fiddlers' gatherings as early as the 1930s. Cleo had won the Missouri State contest at least seven times, as well as capturing the tri-state Missouri, Illinois, Iowa title.

On his final studio album, *Hamilton Ironworks*, John claimed that Cleo had competed against Shorty. Persinger supposedly had gotten roundly beaten by the youngster at the National Oldtime Fiddlers' Contest in Weiser, Idaho, when Shorty was in his early twenties. As John relates on the CD:

> Well, [Cleo Persinger] said one time, "You know, me and the wife, we're going out to Idaho, [and] get in that big old fiddlers' contest out there." And he went out there and, by golly, [when] he come back, he'd won first prize. Next year come by, he says, "I tell you what, I better go out there and defend my championship." Well, he come back, and said, "Aah, I couldn't pull it off this time." Says, "There's a little boy out there and I tell you what, he beat everybody in sight. His name was Texas Shorty. And he and his dad was out there, and they was sellin' records of his fiddlin' out of the trunk of his car." So, Cleo bought one, brought it back home and played it for me. And it's the first time I heard the Texas version of "Dusty Miller." And it's the first time I heard tell of Texas Shorty.

It's true that Cleo Persinger, backed by his wife's guitar playing, competed at Weiser in 1964 and 1965 (the first year for the event was 1953). And newspapers of the day report that Persinger took first place in 1964 and returned the following year to defend his title. However, in 1965, Cleo took sixth, with the top prize awarded *not* to Shorty but to Byron Berline, the Kansas/Oklahoma native who went on to a career as a performer, studio musician, music store owner, and festival promoter. Byron Douglas Berline (1944–2021), who recorded with John's old friends the Dillards in 1965, became as well known to John as Shorty. FYI: Shorty never won the top prize at Weiser, so Cleo may have met him at some other contest in a different location.

Therefore, when and where Persinger purchased the disc from Shorty and played it for John is unknown (Charlie Walden relates that Texas Shorty had visited Cleo in Missouri, leaving behind a stash of Shorty's 45 rpm records). Eventually, John was to acquire all of Shorty's recordings. In later years, John and Shorty became best friends. John would frequently cross paths and jam with Shorty during his travels, often (fortunately for me) in my company.

In 1994 Small Dog also issued *Live at College Station* from a tape recorded by John's soundman/bus driver at a solo John Hartford performance in State College, Pennsylvania. The CD served as a career-spanning greatest-hits collection. The final 1994 release for John's record label was *The Walls We Bounce Off Of.* This solo studio effort was made in response to John's booking agent Keith Case's comment, "Why don't you make an album of funny songs like you used to?" The result is one of my favorite John Hartford albums. Unfortunately, most listeners find the collection an acquired taste. *Walls* owes more of a debt to the Lewis Carroll and Ogden Nash books he read as a youngster than to John's humorous novelty songs of the 1960s and '70s.

In February 1994, John and I finally got to make the fiddle/banjo project instigated several years earlier. I had begun pushing for the endeavor soon after those initial jams in 1991. To secure John's participation, I had to let him set the parameters for the sessions.

For this CD, John drew from his hoard of fiddling resources. Along with music books and manuscripts, John owned an extensive accumulation of private and commercial recordings. He always joked that he was a closet librarian and requested that his personal archive be kept intact after his death and open to the public. Toward that end, the Harford family donated his tune and musical history books to form the John C. Hartford Collection at the Anne Potter Wilson Music Library of the Blair School of Music at Vanderbilt University in Nashville.

After a day of rehearsal, we recorded on the third floor of the Hartford home with his stereo mic plugged into a digital audio tape machine. Over two days, John and I documented what became *The Fun of Open Discussion*. Of the thirty-two tunes in contention, twenty-one were chronicled, with sixteen making the final cut.

Of the pieces included on *The Fun of Open Discussion*, eight John learned from living musicians such as Charlie Acuff ("Kitty Puss"), Ray Knuckles ("Dry and Dusty"), Major Franklin/"Doc" Roberts/ Cyril Stinnett ("Shortenin' Bread"), Johnny Whelan ("Mrs. Maxwell"), Carroll Best ("Chinquapin"), Owen "Snake" Chapman ("Doc Chapman's Breakdown"), Homer Dillard/Howdy Forester/Louie Dunn ("Greenback Dollar"), and Gene Goforth ("Big John McNeil"). An additional four he had gleaned from recordings ("Indian War Whoop," "Bull at the Wagon," "Tishomingo County Blues," and "Hy Patitian"). Two were "book" tunes (from published collections ("Jenny on the Railroad" and "Lantern in the Ditch"), and two more ("The Fun of Open Discussion" and "M.I.S.I.P.") were Hartford originals. John knew Goforth and Knuckles from his home state of Missouri, while Forester and Dunn were Nashville-based players. The other musicians John had met during his performances and at contests, or he sought out after hearing their recordings. These would have included fiddler East Tennessean Charlie Acuff, who John probably first befriended at the Museum of Appalachia, and banjoist Carroll Best of Western North Carolina, who John possibly saw at the Tennessee Banjo Institute.

John approached these recording sessions, as I was to learn, the way he would handle all subsequent sessions with which I was involved. He was always well-rehearsed and had a clear vision for both the repertoire he wanted to pursue as well as the methodology for the session. Although John treated recording seriously, he was relaxed and wanted these projects to be fun for all involved. While I was producing for him, John kept takes to a minimum, although it was unclear if this was a function of his artistic vision or our limited budgets (or both). (I got the impression that John's concurrent recordings with Mark Howard were much more detail oriented and time intensive.)

In my notes accompanying the release, I wrote:

> This recording may surprise fans of John Hartford's music. The less-is-more approach, both in the instrumentation and recording technology utilized, is more akin to John's performances

than to his recent album releases. What may be more startling is John's dedication to the old fiddler's repertoire. And the inclusion of an "old-time" clawhammer style banjoist, downright astonishing!

To those who have been paying close attention to John's career, John Hartford's admiration of pre-bluegrass country music and his love of fiddle music will not come as such a shock. John grew up around old-time and bluegrass fiddling in Missouri, and first performed in those musical styles. Old-time banjoist and original Opry star Uncle Dave Macon contributed the composition "Late Last Night When My Willie Came Home" to John's 1972 release *Morning Bugle*, and Macon was also the source for three pieces on 1992's *Goin' Back to Dixie*. John has contributed articles to *The Devil's Box*, a magazine dedicated to fiddle styles, old and new. John's live shows usually include a fiddle tune or two from the likes of Kentuckian Ed Haley, and bits of traditional melodies infuse many of Hartford's compositions.

John freely admitted that he was prone to extremes, "believing in something 110 percent until I decide to believe in something else." This applied to his approach to everything, including the making of albums. By the time I began supervising John's projects, becoming, as I realize now, his "chief enabler," he had swung back to a faster method of making records—at least, for the ventures deemed "uncommercial" and rejected by the rest of his management team.

Luckily, unlike John's albums made with Jack Clement and Mark Howard, a simple duet recording didn't require any complex arrangements. John was going for spontaneity in our performances and most of the deviations from "just playing the tune" came in either my backups or grew out of our musical interactions.

Although the subsequent albums I recorded with John were all done within the confines of purpose-built recording studios, the approach remained essentially the same as with *Fun*. Partially because of budgetary constraints, but also to maintain a live, spontaneous, and improvised feeling, all our CDs together were cut live, with minimal retakes and overdubs. The musicians played, within eye contact, in one room. Often, different takes were combined to lengthen or improve a performance, while just as frequently, longer pieces were condensed to capture their best moments.

Unfortunately, Marie wasn't convinced that another fiddle record would sell more than the other nonstarters. After the poor showings made by *Old Sport* and *Cadillac Rag*, she chose not to issue *The Fun of Open Discussion* on Small Dog. In fact, every one of John's team—Marie, booking agent Keith Case, and John's accountant Bernie Saul—considered *Fun*, along with all of John's subsequent fiddle-centric recordings of the 1990s, as unimportant/noncommercial side projects and a waste of their time and energy.

Luckily, when I brought the recording to Rounder Records, they disagreed and published the CD. Eventually, John and I would complete four additional albums for Rounder that included his explorations of old-time fiddlers' repertoire as well as John's last collection of original songs. Although none achieved the sales numbers from previous decades, they brought John younger fans and had a profound musical impact.

When *The Fun of Open Discussion* was released at year's end, Bob Buckingham wrote in *Fiddler Magazine*: "These are not traditional fiddle and banjo duets, but a wonderful excursion down a musical side road. Even tunes that are familiar take on new twists that bring new meanings and new feelings to the tune. Each piece, like conversation, evolves from the stated melody."

Even as the sessions for *The Fun of Open Discussion* were completed, John was planning its follow-up. This time, he required a full string band to accompany his fiddle playing. It would be in a new and novel way that only John could conceive, serving to introduce this music to a wider audience than ever before.

CHAPTER THREE

WE JUST GOT BACK FROM JAPAN

I must go down on the levee again, the muddy river and sky
And all I ask is a sternwheel boat and some marks to steer her by
The pull of the wheel, scapin' out on the roof
The pilothouse windows shakin'
A full moon in a Missouri sky, and a foggy morning breaking
—"DOWN ON THE LEVEE"

I've spent the last forty-three years of my life attempting to play the world's two
most despised musical instruments in one of the most unpopular musical styles.
—JOHN HARTFORD

The next stage of my incorporation into John's act came about in
April 1995. At MerleFest, the large-scale musical event staged in North
Carolina, I joined John, Jamie Harford, and bassist Roy Huskey Jr. on
stage for one of their sets. After the performance, John mentioned that
he would be going to Japan at the end of May and needed someone
to back him at concerts, sell merchandise, and road manage for the
short tour. After I blurted out, "What about me?" I was hired. A month
later, I found myself riding John's bus on the way to Jubilee CityFest
in Montgomery, Alabama. After an overnight drive back through
Nashville, the next day John and I performed at the Otter Creek Park
Memorial Bluegrass Festival in Bradenburg, Kentucky. It was then a
relatively short three hours back to Madison.

These two appearances served as trial runs for our upcoming Japanese engagements. After a Sunday at John's house, we were finally on our way overseas.

From the start of our work on *The Fun of Open Discussion*, I had realized that my becoming involved with John in his career could negatively affect our friendship. However, at the time, I felt this was an acceptable trade-off, and therefore continued to insert myself into his music.

John had performed in the Far East once before, taking along Marie Hartford. For him, this second trip was driven purely by promoter demand. He was not in a hurry to return to Asia. It was just a part of his normal life of performing, collecting fees, and heading back home when the tour ended.

In the early spring just before MerleFest, John had cracked his hip, supposedly, as he related it, while playing basketball (I came to believe that the injury was an outcome of his cancer or cancer treatments). As a result, navigating long distances, such as between a terminal check-in desk and boarding gate, proved difficult. When Marie, who had driven us to the Nashville airport, offered to summon a wheelchair, John became angry, as if this was an insult to his manhood. He dug in his heels and insisted on traversing the concourse on his crutches. Luckily, despite the slow passage through the terminal, we had left plenty of time to reach our gate before boarding.

John's refusal to use a wheelchair lasted until our arrival overseas on May 30. When we deplaned at Tokyo's Narita Airport, a young woman assigned by its persons with disabilities department was waiting to meet us. John attempted to refuse once again, but, on this occasion, he had met his match. The attendant not only couldn't understand his English, but, as we gathered, was honor-bound to transport John. She refused to leave without him sitting in the chair.

John begrudgingly seated himself and was surprised how easily we traversed through customs and immigration. For all intents and purposes, John and I were waved through the VIP sections. The funniest exchange I had was with a customs agent. When asked why we were traveling with hundreds of CDs and T-shirts, I replied as I was instructed (untruthfully, as they were to be sold at our concerts):

"They're for promotional purposes." Although he looked at me strangely, John and I passed without paying any duty on our merchandise.

When we arrived back in the United States upon the conclusion of the trip, John once again took to a wheelchair. And, as before, our quick passage through customs and immigration (which included being greeted by a security guard as, "It's the steamboat captain") caused John to comment that "from now on, one of the band's [members] will always be in a wheelchair" to assure a speedy passage through airports. (Unfortunately, it didn't always work.)

John and I spent three days in Tokyo. Our visit was capped with two appearances on June 1 at the Rocky Top club, which held about seventy-five people. We were well cared for in the city, and all of our trip, by Japanese bluegrass musicians.

During the first half of our short tour, John and I were chauffeured by Masuo Sasabe, one of the top bluegrass singers and guitarists in Japan. For our first night in town, Masuo picked us up at Narita and took us for conveyer belt sushi in the Ginza. He then delivered us to a typical upscale Japanese businessman's hotel in a sedate part of the city. Although this was by far the fanciest accommodation during our trip, these lodgings were conceived for Japanese patrons and not designed for Western tastes. The small rooms were fine with me, although the bathrooms took a bit of adjustment.

While my wife was raised in Seattle around a significant Japanese population and well-versed in their cuisine, I had never ventured into an establishment serving sushi. I was living (and still live) in rural North Carolina, where our local health department strongly advised against eating raw food overseas. However, I ignored that warning when Masuo took us to eat our first night in Tokyo. From that point on, any food I was brought I would try, with John being just a bit less adventurous.

Since 1985 when our friendship had commenced, I had mostly seen the positive side of John's personality. True, I was witness to some angry outbursts. But they were directed at others, as with his refusal of wheelchairs in the airport. As I was to intuit, often John used these emotional outbursts as a bargaining tactic to get his way with promoters, record producers, and the like.

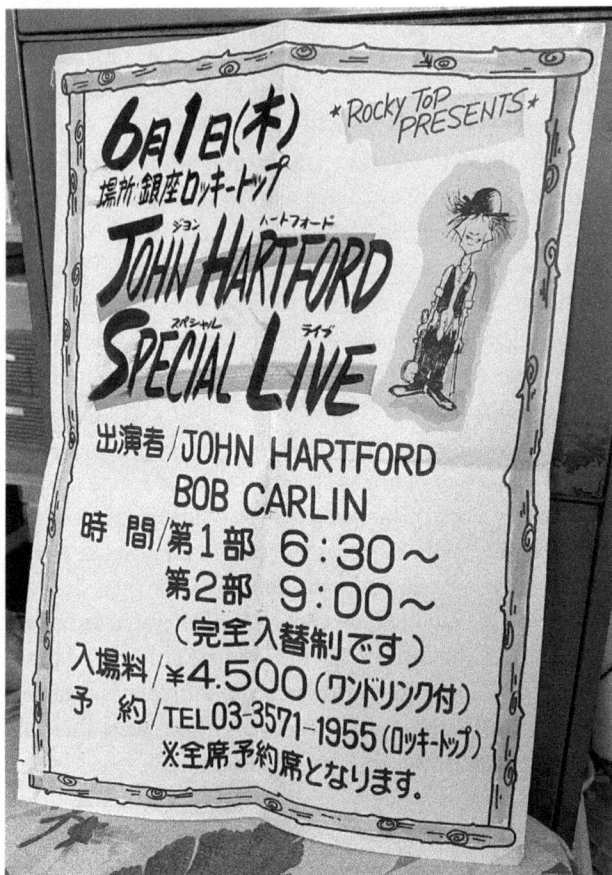

Poster, Rocky Top Club, Tokyo, Japan, June 1, 1995. Caricature of John Hartford drawn by himself taken from the cover art for his CD, *The Walls We Bounce Off Of* (Small Dog A-Barkin' Records). Collection of the author. My first "official" performances backing John occurred in the spring of 1995, with four appearances in Japan. This is the poster from our concert in Tokyo.

During this sojourn, I saw John dig in his heels at our hotel. Upon check-in, it became evident that we had been booked into the same room. In John's defense, he didn't get angry, just insistent. Thankfully, this was an occasion where his refusal quickly converted the arrangements into two separate rooms. (I think relations would have quickly broken down sharing one space, although we successfully stayed together on future occasions. However, those were for only a few nights at a time.) As you'll gather from this account, our daily routines outside of the concerts were so different that we couldn't have survived cohabitation.

In Tokyo, as for the other stops on the tour, the posters and advertisements showed us as an equally billed act. Since these were John Hartford concerts, and I was just his accompanist, this was an unexpected move by the promoters. As we had just come out with a duo album, I could justify the origins for this confusion. However, where I viewed the joint billing as a misunderstanding, John, somewhat understandably, took it as a personal affront. Unfortunately, this led him to angrily accuse me (falsely and absurdly) of contacting the sponsors behind his back and arranging to be included in the concert credits (which, of course, I hadn't). This billing continued to be an irritant for him throughout our travels in Japan.

In his defense, following that promotional mishap, I only remember John angrily dressing me down twice more during this trip. Both times were also due to misunderstandings and misreadings of offstage situations. And, during the following seven years that we worked together, the additional times he yelled at me were few. This was remarkable, as I'm sure I tried his patience on many other occasions.

For the duration of our stay, John quickly settled into a routine. Some of his habits might have been dictated by the limitations imposed by the hip injury that placed John on crutches. This also eliminated his ability to stand and dance for the performances.

Determined to remain on Nashville time, he would stay up all night in his hotel room (conveniently located next to mine) practicing his fiddling (which I, and, therefore, all the other guests, could plainly hear). However, we never were told of a complaint from staff or other travelers, possibly due to the polite mores of Japanese society. This acceptance, whether based upon his celebrity or Japanese custom or both, followed John for the rest of the tour. John's eccentric and sometimes embarrassing provocations received no response from sponsors and audiences alike. However, I was not granted the same "pass" by the Japanese. Even though I worked hard at respecting the customs of our hosts, everything I did seemed to prompt embarrassed responses. I just couldn't do anything right.

Seated: John Hartford. Standing l to r: Hisataka Koshida, Yasuhisa Kato, Bob Carlin, Masuo Sasabe, Tetsu Shimomura. Jamming at our Tokyo appearance with some of our Japanese hosts. Rocky Top club, Tokyo, Japan, June 1, 1995. Collection of the author.

Right when the hotel restaurant opened in the morning, I would be summoned to accompany John downstairs to eat. He would order an American breakfast, usually with a steak. The first morning in Tokyo, I was woken by John several hours before the cafe opened. I sleepily explained he'd have to wait, that I had no control over their hours, and returned to my bed.

By 9:00 a.m., Masuo would arrive to pick us up for several hours of sightseeing. Following lunch, John would retire to his bed for an afternoon of sleep. Excited for the opportunity, I would investigate the local landmarks and culture. I toured temples, visited the large Sony store downtown, and journeyed to the Tokyo professional baseball stadium, the Big Egg. In the evenings, after another meal, John would either hold a jam session with local musicians or play a concert.

The only change to our schedule came on travel days, or when John had his interest piqued. Once, he saw a Westerner on the street wearing a vest John admired. Being obviously a fancier of vests himself, John approached the man about where one could be obtained. After finding it was acquired from a local shop, we were quickly on our way to facilitate his own purchase.

While we were overseas and still at the beginning of our trip, John was captivated by the writing system called kanji. Masuo graciously took us to a large Tokyo bookstore that specialized in English language materials so that John could purchase a volume on this style of written Japanese language. In this store, local shoppers kept coming up to me, wanting to practice their English skills.

From there, it was on to Hiratsuka for a concert in the ballroom of the Hotel Sunroute, which was also where we stayed. On our way, Masuo took us to meet a friend of his, Shinji Kojima. Shinji owned a sushi restaurant in Yokohama named Sushizanmai. The outside was covered with driftwood and the inside had a bar with room for fewer than ten patrons. As we walked in, the sounds of classic American country music played on the hi-fi, and Shinji's resophonic guitar rested in the rafters above the open kitchen.

For someone unacquainted with sushi, that day I received a full-scale introduction/initiation into a range of dishes. We found out later from Masuo, who graciously covered our meals, that his friend didn't have set prices but charged depending on how much he liked you. Since Hartford was revered by Japanese musicians, we were served as honored guests on ceramic roof tiles native to Yokohama and billed about half of what other patrons normally paid.

John's performance in Hiratsuka, held within a large banquet room at the hotel, was promoted, I believe, by a local music store, Banjo Boy's Old Guitar Shop. The store was owned by Yasuhiro "Taco" Ohmori. As I recall, they were our local contact and took care of us. They also transported us to our next gig in Tokiyama.

For the Japanese shows, John played banjo, fiddle, guitar, and sang, which I, per John's instructions, backed up with simple bass lines and chords on the banjo. This was different from my normal playing style, which sketches the melody of the fiddle, as well as providing support and counterpoint to its rhythm. At the time, I thought just playing bass lines sounded insipid; at the least, I found it very unsatisfying. I didn't understand what John was after. However, listening back to those shows twenty-five years later, more often than not my playing worked surprisingly well with John's music. I was to eventually learn

John Hartford (l) and Bob Carlin at our second Japanese concert, Hotel Sunroute, Hiratsuka, Japan, June 2, 1995. Collection of the author.

that, as I explain whenever discussing John and his music, that 50 percent of what John did was genius and 50 percent was unsuccessful (not unusual for the creative output of any artist). Unfortunately, in the moment, it was impossible to separate the brilliance from the nonsense. So, I learned to just accept and support it all and, in time, it would become obvious which ideas worked and which didn't.

The set list from the Hotel Sunroute was pretty standard for John Hartford shows during this period. Most of the original material came from John's recordings of the 1980s and '90s. These included the love songs "Learning to Smile All Over Again" and "All in My Love for You," along with the fiddle instrumental "Ohio River Rag" (*Annual Waltz*); "More Big Bull Fiddle Fun" and the banjo instrumental "Your Tax Dollars at Work" (*The Walls We Bounce Off Of*); as well as "Here I Am in Love Again" and the novelty blues progression "Bring Your Clothes Back Home" (*Down on the River*). Fiddle tunes were sprinkled throughout; as instrumentals, they transcended the language difference.

During the first set, sensing a hesitancy on the part of those in attendance, John attempted some audience participation. To relax the crowd, John also threw in a run of bluegrass standards. These included "Groundhog," "Wabash Cannonball," and "Tennessee Waltz." Of course, it wouldn't have been a night of John Hartford without his "hits" "Gentle on My Mind" and "Steam Powered Aereo Plane." All followed his performing philosophy of "play one of theirs" (discussed in chapter 4).

John's Japanese fans treated his performances like sacred events. This was most obvious at the Sunroute, where the audience was generally older and more sedate than at our other concerts. However, at the "meet and greet" after the show, I saw many fans reduced to tears of joy when they got to meet John. This was probably due to an overly reverential response to one of their musical heroes standing in front of them.

After the Sunroute, we spent two days at the Mountain Time Acoustic Music Festival in Tokiyama, north of Nagoya. The drive took us past stunning mountain views, on hillsides covered with tea bushes, through a light mist that turned into a cold, steady rain. A quick afternoon nap in a local home was followed by a wild indoor concert at the campground's gymnasium. It ended with John, probably playing "Orange Blossom Special" on the fiddle, calling and leading the assembled masses in an impromptu square dance.

For that evening, we were to be housed by a glass blower, who lived in a modern Japanese-style structure nearby. However, John decided to stay at the festival grounds and jam all night in the campground. When I awoke the next morning, it was to the sound of temple bells and superb scenery. While John slept through Sunday, June 4, our host drove me to a pottery so I could purchase a piece to bring back to my wife Rachel, a ceramic artist. I had brought along some small samples of her work, and I gifted him with one, as I had been doing for our other facilitators during the trip (this followed Japanese tradition). I then rode with fiddler "Bosco" Takaki, who had attended the festival, back to his home in Kyoto, where I was to spend the rest of Sunday and Monday. I continued my break from John by touring the historic part of the city, visiting a record store, and eating udon (a type of noodle) for the first time. The udon restaurant used a very particular style of flawed handmade Japanese pottery, which, in my ignorance, I thought were damaged rejects. My wife later educated me about wabi-sabi, the art of appreciating the beauty of imperfect, asymmetrical objects formed by humans that let the materials dictate the form.

After the time off in Kyoto, it was on to Osaka for one final concert. John and I performed at a shuttered discotheque named Another Dream in the basement of our hotel. In the city, I drank very expensive but high-quality boutique coffee (this was before the Starbucksification of the beverage) and witnessed the only street people, graffiti, trash, and pornography shops that I saw in Japan. The porno stores should have clued me in to the hotel being in a red-light district. It all became apparent the evening of our performance. As I rode between the venue and my hotel room, I shared the elevator with a succession of businessmen in suits with well-dressed women in short skirts and very high heels.

The performance was packed and exciting as we all shared the knowledge that this would be John's last concert in Japan. Nothing stands out about the actual show, except for the disco ball suspended from the ceiling!

After the appearance, at my instigation, the Japanese bluegrass mandolinist Shin Akimoto introduced John and me to his shamisen instructor. I had been attempting to learn about the Okinawan lute instrument through recordings and was very excited to see one played in person. It was then on to the Osaka airport and back to Nashville.

Thus began my employment as a member of John's back-up musical corps, which lasted until his untimely passing in 2001.

One of the influences on John resulting from our travels in Japan were his new way of introducing his concerts. Language and the nuances contained in spoken and written interjections had fascinated him since his youth. John also was impressed by the difficulty of conveying meaning to Japanese speakers of English. The misunderstandings one could have communicating, and the way intent changed through translation, were brought home to John while abroad.

Overseas, John began thanking his audiences in "pigeon" Japanese. "Arigatōgozaimashita," which loosely translates into English as "thank you," became "Dobro oregano" in Johnspeak. John thought this extremely funny, although, from the lack of listener response, I believe that none of his Japanese fans understood him enough to get the joke or to take offense.

After the penultimate appearance in Japan, John and I posed for photographs with mandolinist Shin Akimoto and his shamisen instructor, as well as some other Japanese string musicians. Front row, l to r: John Hartford, Masao Koshima, Bob Carlin. Back row, l to r: Shin Akimoto, Yasutaka Adachi, Bosco Takaki. Another Dream club, Osaka, Japan, June 6, 1995. Collection of the author.

Once back in the United States, John began utilizing an introduction motivated by his experiences in Japan with language barriers. Within a day of our return, when John and I stood onstage at Mark O'Connor's fiddle camp outside of Nashville, John spoke the words that he would immortalize for the rest of his life. With some improvised variation, he told the audience how he was "tickled to death" to be there. John continued that we had "just got back from Japan," where John informed his fans that he was "tickled to death" to be there—which was translated, according to John, into Japanese as "he scratches himself until he dies." This invariably got a big laugh from American audiences.

Another manifestation of our foreign trip motivated John several years later to have his notes for Chris Sharp's CD translated into Japanese and then back into English. Unfortunately, the desired effect of transforming their meaning into something comical was not achieved and the idea was abandoned.

You're either on the bus or off the bus.
—KEN KESEY

The Japanese tour was my introduction to traveling with John, both on the bus and by other means of transport. Originally, we were to journey between our start in Tokyo and finish in Osaka by train. This appeared in my limited experience to be the standard way that many touring musicians in Japan moved from one appearance to another. However, because of John's limited mobility, we ended up traveling by automobile between each engagement. Although I was provided some travel information in advance, by and large, while overseas we relied on the goodwill of others to get to where we needed to be on time.

What was impressed upon me during the Japanese tour and continued once I began traveling more with John on his bus was how chaotic and unplanned arrangements appeared. John seemingly didn't bother himself with anything other than performing his show and collecting payment. He left all the other details—where the gig was located, directions on how to get there, what were the expectations of the promoter, where were we staying—to others. For those times on his bus, it was the driver and, eventually, me who he trusted to know all the particulars. When without his bus, John mostly kept his own counsel and let whoever decided to road manage handle the specifics. John always used to say something to the effect that, "I put myself in the chute and assume everything will eventually happen as planned," a mantra he had used since his earliest days flying between gigs. Since I couldn't trust anyone within his organization to inform the band of the travel details, I eventually made it my priority to know all that minutiae before we left Nashville.

Papaw drives Mamaw around the country in a big silver bus so she can shop.

When John first entered show business, he traveled to gigs (as did many novices) in a Volkswagen automobile. Once John was based in California, he would rehearse and videotape the Smothers Brothers and Glen Campbell programs on weekdays and then fly to his weekend engagements. John's travel by airplane continued throughout the 1970s. He once bragged that he flew without a road manager, carrying all his instruments and luggage himself. I remember seeing John at the Philadelphia Folk Festival running toward the stage before his set and away from the stage immediately afterwards with all his belongings strapped onto him. During those years of solo travel, John claims to have only ever missed one gig. He fell asleep on a plane, failed to make his connection, and ended up in the wrong city.

Eventually, in emulation of his bluegrass heroes, John bought himself his own tour bus. From 1980 onward, he mostly traveled to engagements on that vehicle. First, John purchased a Golden Eagle. He upgraded to two Silver Eagles that were then welded together to elongate and enlarge the living space. The Eagles were converted from retired passenger buses into recreational vehicles. Unfortunately, the extended length of the Silver Eagle constantly caused problems with the linkage and transmission.

Accompanying John on his travels was Marie, who handled the sales of merchandise at appearances. (Marie's granddaughter once quipped, "Papaw drives Mamaw around the country in a big silver bus so she can shop.") John also utilized his touring to visit and jam with a large extended network of friends and associates in the music and riverboat communities.

Someone had to drive the vehicle, and the operators that John engaged were also expected to road manage, set up the stage, as well as run sound for his appearances. The list of John's main bus drivers includes Joe Hutson (early 1980s), Roger Jackson and relief driver Lem Kinslow (1985–89), Tim Wendt (1988, 1992–95), Jerry McCoury (1995–96), Darrin Vincent (1996–97), Jimmy Johnson (1997–98), Mike Compton (relief driver early 1990s–1998, lead driver 1998–2000), and Larry Perkins (1998–2001).

All these men (and drivers were primarily if not exclusively male) had been lured into bus driving through their pursuit of the music profession. Just before working for John, Lem Kinslow had been a member of the Monitors Quartet gospel group. Tim Wendt, an expert operator trained on farm and other heavy machinery, had moved to Nashville to pursue a career as a performer. McCoury, the younger brother of singer/bandleader Del McCoury, had formerly been a musician with Don Reno and Red Smiley. Jerry had become weary of touring and retired to raise a family back home in Pennsylvania. Jerry McCoury moved to Nashville for a second attempt at the music profession. However, there was too much tension between his family life and life on the road, so, after a year or so, Jerry once again returned home to Pennsylvania. Darrin Vincent came from a musical clan (he is the younger brother of Rhonda Vincent). Darrin has since achieved fame as a member of Ricky Skaggs' Kentucky Thunder as well as in a duo with Jamie Dailey. Jimmy Johnson played guitar with an array of country talent, including Leroy Van Dyke, and was also known as a songwriter. Mike Compton and Larry Perkins were members of the second Hartford Stringband.

When one boarded the Frankenstein Silver Eagle, you passed between the driver and navigator's seats through two blackout curtains drawn to facilitate privacy and night driving. Down the aisle flanked by two sleeping couches (each also with drapes) was a small kitchen area. Past the kitchen sat a bathroom/shower on the navigator's side and a curtained bunk bed on the driver's side. The aisle ended at a door, through which was located the master bedroom over the engine. There were various closets, cabinets, and bins for storage situated throughout the vehicle.

In the second half of the 1980s, blues guitarist Roy Book Binder appeared on many of the same shows as John and remembers how John Hartford's bus gained a shower. Roy and his first wife were visiting with John and Marie, with Roy and John on John's bus and the two spouses in Roy's motor home. After seeing Roy's bathroom set-up, Marie demanded the addition from John.

There were many advantages to traveling by bus. It was self-contained and afforded John the ability to replicate as closely as possible his home work environment. He could carry a lot more of his tune books, recordings, and instruments than if he were traveling by airplane. The amount of transferring your belongings from conveyance to hotel bedrooms was also limited. The best part of bus travel was that the musicians could get a full night's sleep after a gig and (mostly) wake up at the location of the next engagement or back at home. As I informed *Old Time Herald* interviewer Gail Gillespie about my time with John: "You can't beat a bus when you're at some muddy festival. You've got a bathroom and a shower and a dry bed to lie down on!"

As John informed *Radio Times*' host Marty Moss-Cohane in 1988:

> I love the road; I like to travel, and I like to play. I try to put what I make back into being comfortable on the road because that's where I spend most of my time. So, I don't make much money on the road because my overhead is so high. But at least I'm comfortable and I'm healthy.

Obviously, there were disadvantages to bus travel. You had to sleep with your feet toward the front so that, in event of a crash, one would only break a leg, not the neck. Privacy was also a big issue, as the small space meant that everyone was constantly in each other's business.

Although John's drivers were expert at maneuvering the tour vehicle around tight spaces, they had their share of mishaps. For John's first Eagle, there was the occasion when its height prohibited entering an airport, which necessitated the removal of one of the air conditioning units from the roof. The bus had to return home with a large opening in the top where the AC had lived.

Over the years, there were additional tight spots. Several times when I was with John, the drivers backed into and/or damaged other vehicles. On one occasion, performing for the *Mountain Stage* radio program at a ski resort in Snowshoe, West Virginia, the bus was reversed into fellow musician Leon Redbone's rented van. On another trip, we pulled the fender off a car belonging to one of the band's friends! There were also scary travels over ice-covered highways, as well as brushes with other drivers forcing us onto the grassy median of a freeway.

There were some humorous times on the road as well. One of the drivers during the 1990s had a terrible sense of direction. By that time, as I had become the road manager, I was often called upon to navigate whenever he got lost (which was often). On another occasion, with Larry Perkins at the wheel, we took the bus through a drive-through of a fast-food restaurant (it actually fit). We managed to thoroughly frighten the staff, who thought we were a passenger bus filled with tourists rather than a tour bus with only five musicians on board.

My favorite occasion was when we left the aforementioned Larry Perkins behind at a truck stop in Kentucky (well, not a favorite occasion for him). Larry had just finished his driving shift, stripped to a pair of shorts, and gotten into one of the bunk beds for some sleep. With Mike Compton behind the wheel, we stopped to get something to eat. Initially, just Mike and I got off, leaving (we thought) a sleeping Larry and John behind. When John changed his mind and exited the vehicle to pick up a sandwich, Larry woke up and told John he was getting off as well. When Mike and I got back on the bus, John didn't say anything, so we assumed that Larry was still asleep in his bed. An hour down the highway, the bus was pulled over by the highway patrol. The policeman approached the bus and asked us if we knew a Larry Perkins. This prompted an "Oh, shit" from John and, assuming Perkins was in the patrol car, laughter from me and Mike. Unfortunately for Larry, after the bus had pulled away and left him standing in his shorts, the policeman wouldn't bring him to rendezvous with us. After driving the hour back to get him, a visibly angry Larry Perkins got back into his bunk and went to sleep.

Our travel routines followed some broad outlines. Although the length of the trip usually determined our departure time, the preferred method was to drive at night when the traffic was lightest, and the band could sleep. Therefore, we'd wake up in the morning close to or at our destination. Most of the time, since the bus and everyone but me lived in the Nashville area, we'd depart from there. On some occasions, I'd meet the bus along the route either at a truck stop, or, if I flew, in an airport. I also drove my vehicle to some appearances.

During the evening, we would make fuel stops, read, talk, practice, or watch movies, among other activities. Our routine was to stay up as late as one could to fall asleep more easily. During the time of the Stringband, the couch behind the driver was mine, with Chris Sharp on the one behind the "navigator's" seat. The drivers occupied the bunk beds farther back, with John in the master bedroom at the rear.

Whenever we arrived near our destination, the bus was generally parked behind a Cracker Barrel restaurant. There were several reasons for that location. One, the restaurant had ample bus parking. Two, Cracker Barrels were located near interstate highways. And three, those who wanted to sleep could sleep, such as the driver, who had been up all night. And the others could easily walk into Cracker Barrel and eat when they desired.

When we were parked in a location where band members could access restaurants, often, everyone went his separate way. When meal choices were limited or we had to find the proper interstate exit with eateries, John would often dictate where we would stop. Used to getting what he wanted whenever he wanted it, John would often make unrealistic requests, which generally I had to help satisfy. As an example, I remember one late-night desire in the middle of the rural upper Midwest for sushi.

As I was probably the most adventurous gourmand in the band and certainly had the widest experience searching for options on the road, I was often called upon by John to find a specific cuisine. This often led to some meals that were a cut above what was eaten by most bluegrass bands. This included stops in Madison, Wisconsin, for Japanese food and escargot in Maine. When the venues provided a repast, it was often serviceable but unmemorable. One exception occurred in Salt Lake City. Because we flew to Utah and were performing downtown, the band was housed in the Hotel Monaco, a boutique hotel within a historic bank building near the venue. The performers were given carte blanche for the first-floor restaurant—anything we wanted to eat off the elegant menu was comped by our hosts.

In the words of author Ken Kesey, I was now officially "on the bus," and a member of John's musical ensemble.

> Most of what I do is not career building.
> —JOHN HARTFORD, TO DAVID HOLT

As the 1990s progressed, John's income per performance dropped, as did his total number of concerts. His tour vehicle aged, increasing John's travel expenses with the resulting lowering of his net profits. John took on additional musicians, which also increased the cost of touring. As John continued to lose money, both Marie and John's accountant, Bernie Saul, tried to dissuade him from performing, to no avail. Against the continuing recommendations of his family and financial team, John persisted in subsidizing his music and these travels with income from his songwriting royalties and investments.

John's desire in the 1990s to underwrite his music making appears, in retrospect, to have sprung from his illness. Others, including myself, have commented that once this bout of cancer appeared to be life threatening, John decided to devote the remainder of his life to making music. This encompassed performing and recording as much as was allowed by his weakened physical and psychological state.

While John was raised in comfort, Marie appeared to have had a hardscrabble upbringing. She was a great lover of bargains, and incessantly clipped coupons and watched her spending. John was not a spendthrift but liked creature comforts and disbursed money on things that were important to him, like meals, books, and recordings.

Being family-oriented, Marie always worried about her children and grandchildren (these were from previous unions, not John's biological children). Like a stereotypical mother hen, she always guarded their well-being. Therefore, with John determined to outspend his earnings from performances by dipping into their savings, his wife did everything she could to stem his outpourings of cash. Marie once stated in my presence that she could live on nothing, that didn't worry her. However, she needed to provide for her offspring as she was certain (whether rightly or wrongly) that at least some of them were unable to care for themselves or their children.

Eventually, when it came to the tour bus, John and Marie became, as the saying goes, pennywise and pound foolish. Less and less money was put into maintaining the vehicle, and it continually broke down. Ultimately, the Hartfords spent more repairing the bus than if they had properly maintained it or replaced it with a newer model. Another effect on John and his musicians were missed gigs and becoming stranded away from home while the vehicle was being repaired. To fill in the gaps when the Eagle was out of commission, Marie's van or air travel were pressed into service to convey the band between engagements.

PUT ANY OLD NAME ON ANY OLD RHYME.

Following our tour of Japan, because I was not yet integrated into John's full-time touring group, the performances where I accompanied him were local to Nashville and/or low-fee gigs that John took for enjoyment. These included a concert at Mark O'Connor's fiddle camp; the fiddle contest at the Appalachian String Band Festival in Clifftop, West Virginia (where John placed third); a tribute to fiddler Benny Sims at Bristol's Paramount Theater in Tennessee; and the Celebration of Traditional Music at Berea College in Kentucky.

Along with fellow researcher Brandon Kirk, John had been invited to the Berea festival to share information about his current obsession, Blind Ed Haley, and to perform Haley's music in the evening concerts. These included several pieces fiddled by Ed on home recordings, as well as a number of tunes that Haley was thought to have played. John would record the latter group the following year for what became the album *Wild Hog in the Red Brush*.

Born James Edward Haley in 1883 in Logan County, West Virginia, an attack of measles at an early age left Ed blind. He began playing music as a child, meeting and marrying his life companion, Martha Ella Crumbs, another sightless musician, around the time of World War I. The couple settled in Ashland, Kentucky, where they raised a family and traveled the region making music. When Ed and Ella's son Ralph returned from the Army Signal Corps after World War II, he purchased a home disc-cutting machine and extensively recorded his father's fiddling.

In 1976, Rounder Records issued fourteen of these recordings on LP. Even though he had never heard of Ed Haley, John purchased the disc because it had a fiddler on the front cover and a steamboat on the back (two of the things that John loved). This album initiated John's obsession with the music of Ed Haley.

As John stated in the many interviews he gave during the last ten years of his life, he was "eat up" with Ed Haley's music. From the early 1990s until his death in 2001, John dedicated his life to finding out everything he could about Ed. A fuller group of Ed Haley's own recordings were eventually released by Rounder Records on a pair of two-CD sets under John's direction and my supervision. And, beginning in 1995, he made an alliance with Brandon to assemble a manuscript about Ed Haley's life and music.

The two devoted years to research, with Brandon focusing on genealogy and archival searches, while John interviewed musicians and others who knew Haley. Eventually, Brandon moved to Nashville, hired by John to help write the Ed Haley story. His salary was justified by Marie through employing him to help grandson Dustin attain his GED certification.

John and Brandon assembled several versions of a manuscript, which they titled *In Search of Ed Haley*. However, work on the book ended with the collapse of Brandon's marriage and his move back to his childhood home in rural West Virginia.

In the years that John and Brandon worked together, a close relationship developed between the two men. John regarded him as he would a son. In some ways, he was closer to Brandon Kirk then he was to his own children.

John never recovered from Brandon Kirk's sudden departure. The last time the two were in the same room, John was living his last days in the hospital. Heavily sedated, he may or may not have been aware that Brandon was present.

At John's invitation, I monitored the progress of the two men's Ed Haley investigation, and often read the various versions they produced. The resulting texts reflected two very distinct styles of writing. While Brandon composed like an academic, in dense, statistic-driven prose, John created a more informal, conversational narrative. As I do not currently have access to the manuscript, an excerpt utilized in John's notes for the Ed Haley reissues will serve as an example of John's writing style:

> Lawrence [Haley] was at home one day after the original Rounder album came out and a man knocked on his door and said he had some discs of Ed's music he would trade for one of the *Parkersburg Landing* albums. Lawrence agreed.... We [John always referred to himself in the plural within his writings] also tracked down and got some records from Dr. Holbrook in Ashland that just weren't clear enough to use and after you hear some of what we did use, you'll realize just how bad they are.

Unfortunately, John decided to structure the book as, literally, the story of his personal search for information about Haley. Toward that end, he arranged all the information he had gathered (and, I mean, *all* the information) in the chronological order in which he had found it. This resulted in a long and repetitive tale. On page five, John would tell you he went to see (for example) Wilson Douglas, who told him Ed Haley wore a long wool overcoat even in the summer. Five pages later, John visited Lawrence Haley, who commented that his father wore a long wool overcoat even in the summer, and smoked a pipe. Page twenty-five repeated the same information, with one additional tidbit, and this type of repetition occurs throughout the narrative.

At some point after there was a finished draft of *In Search of Ed Haley* (I cannot remember whether this occurred before or after John passed), I had a series of meetings with Vanderbilt University Press. This may have occurred after John's death, because I worked for his estate before it passed to the Harford family. One of Vanderbilt's junior editors was extremely interested in acquiring the book. Because we both deemed the current version difficult to digest by most readers, I suggested that Vanderbilt publish an edited account and include a DVD containing John's original manuscript.

Vanderbilt was headed toward signing John and Brandon's story when something occurred internally at the Press, and our discussions were ended. As far as I know, beside the excerpts John used for his notes to the Ed Haley CD releases, and some in Brandon Kirk's book *Blood in West Virginia*, the full version is yet unpublished.

When John decided to issue the Haley discs on CD, I made sure that I was involved in the process. As I told Gail Gillespie of the *Old Time Herald*:

At the time, I was Hartford's project director for recordings, and I insinuated myself into the CD project because I saw that there was a recipe for disaster! John very much wanted to see the Ed Haley recordings come out, but he certainly didn't have the technical knowledge to oversee the transfers and processing so that they would sound the best that they could.

So, because I had a relationship with him and because I also had one with Rounder Records, I got myself hired and eventually ended up supervising the sound and directing the project for Rounder.

It's also important to emphasize that, without John behind the project, Rounder would never have done four CDs worth of Ed Haley's music. And John had the clout to demand that Rounder pay for state-of-the-art transfers and mastering.

In the spring and summer of 1996, I redubbed the Haley discs at the Southern Folklife Collection of the University of North Carolina at Chapel Hill. Audio engineer Dave Glasser did the equalization and noise reduction at Airshow Mastering, leading to the release of the first two-CD set in the summer of 1997. The second two-disc collection followed a year later.

Throughout the winter of 1995, John tried out a number of pieces he was considering for his own tribute to Haley's fiddling. Jamie Harford and I provided the accompaniment on these work tapes. Lawrence Haley, Ed's youngest son, had entrusted John with the surviving home recordings of his father's fiddling. In March, Bruce Nemerov from the Center for Popular Music at Middle Tennessee State University in Murfreesboro provided fresh dubs of Ralph Haley's discs. This collection further encouraged John's study of Ed Haley's playing.

At first, John focused on replicating the versions of the tunes played by the master fiddler on these recordings. However, intimidated by the prospect of being compared to Haley's originals, John chose instead to assemble a playlist from those attempted by Ed Haley that weren't found within the grooves of the home discs. Since Marie still looked unfavorably on any fiddle collection for Small Dog, I approached Rounder Records, who had released John's and my previous collaboration, *The Fun of Open Discussion*. Luckily, Rounder agreed to underwrite the project.

A year later, John was finally ready to record. As opposed to the simple fiddle/banjo duo utilized for *The Fun of Open Discussion*, for *Wild Hog* John wanted a full-blown string band to render his Haley interpretations. The Hartford String Band [sic] name John had utilized in the 1980s (informally, he labeled us "The Leakage Seekers") was revived. For the sessions, he gathered mandolinist Mike Compton and bassist Jerry McCoury from his touring outfit, with Jerry's nephew Ronnie McCoury—himself an acclaimed member of his father Del's group—on guitar, and me on banjo to accompany his fiddling.

After a day of rehearsal, the ensemble convened on the last day of January and the first day of February 1996 at Mark Howard's Eleven-O-Three Studio. I was coproducer with John, as with *Fun*, and we chose to record and mix the project in Nashville.

There were several "affects" that John utilized for these recordings. First (perhaps, in a reference to field recordings), he wanted to sing/announce the titles to the tunes before playing them. Secondly, John employed an early version of a method he eventually came to label "windows." John had been told by Irish fiddler Kevin Burke that jazz trumpeter Wynton Marsalis believed "Most of the revolutions in popular music really are made in the rhythm section," and "windows" grew out of that assumption (I have not been able to verify that Marsalis actually promoted this theory). This was John's method of varying the backup in ways he hoped would make fiddle music more interesting and acceptable to a wider public. The responsibility for "arranging" each tune was passed in turn around the circle of musicians. Hand signals were utilized to bring each player in and out of the performance. On the resulting CD, John repeatedly fiddles the tune at hand while the mandolin, banjo, guitar, and bass weave a musical tapestry around him, alternately playing lead, rhythm, counterpoint, and bass lines—or not playing at all. John's final words of advice to the band were, "As long as you start and end on the right note, it doesn't matter what you play in between."

With a relaxed and informal atmosphere, thirty-two takes were made the first day and twenty-two the second. A total of twenty-two fiddle tunes and two songs were committed to digital tape. Most of the second day was spent on retakes, along with focusing on the two songs about Haley's family history that went unissued.

Eventually, the session broke down into a jam. John ended the proceedings with the exclamation, "There you have it, folks. You boys did a good job."

Wild Hog in the Red Brush was released to wonderful acclaim. County Sales called the recording "Fine," and they chose it as one of the best fiddle recordings of 1996. The album received a Grammy nomination, the first of John's instrumental albums to gain such an honor.

Musician Chris Coole wrote in *The Old Time News* of his first exposure to the "windows" recordings by John and the Stringband:

When I started listening to the album, I was taken a bit off-guard as it was unlike anything I'd ever heard before. I was used to old-time backup that while driving, was very "consistent" in its support of the fiddle. There would maybe be the odd edgy bass-run on the guitar, but for the most part the band would provide a steady rhythmic bed for the fiddle to play on and there wasn't a lot of tension, rhythmically or tonally, between the band and the fiddle.

On *Wild Hog* the band seemed to be endlessly "jamming" behind the fiddle. To my ears, it never seemed to get settled. It wasn't that the rhythm wasn't locked in, it's just that it was more fluid than I was accustomed to and the texture of it always seemed to be changing.

Although, on the first few listens the music almost seemed chaotic to me, I was very quickly drawn in and won over. There was something about the way the band was playing behind Hartford that made the music come alive in a way that I'd never heard before in an old-time stringband. Good music is always a conversation between the musicians playing it, but that fact seemed to be on "overdrive" on this album. The musicians really seemed to be playing off each other. There was always something to listen to, and something new seemed to be revealed on each listen as you peeled away the layers. It was some of the most engaging old-time music I'd ever heard.

Around the same time as the release of *Wild Hog in the Red Brush*, John also chose to issue his latest collection of original songs on Small Dog, *No End of Love*. The title composition and his revised version of "Gentle on My Mind" (see chapter 4) were originally from 1967's *Earthwords & Music* (RCA Victor). The remainder of the album focused on new Hartford lyrics. Preceded by spoken introductions, each song spun a story involving a historic riverboat. In many ways, this collection was the logical extension of his 1986 book *Steamboat in a Cornfield*. Backing John for this Mark Howard production were Jamie Harford on vocals, Roy Huskey on bass and two of the *Wild Hog* band, Ronnie McCoury on guitar and Mike Compton on mandolin.

L to r: Bob Carlin, Mike Compton, John Hartford. Tennessee Fall Homecoming, Museum of Appalachia, Norris, TN, October 10–13, 1996. Yet another occasion where I sat in with John and his touring band: Mike Compton on mandolin and (not shown) Darrin Vincent, who followed Jerry McCoury in John's group on bass. Although I was working with John on recordings and other projects, I only occasionally appeared onstage for concerts by the Hartford band. Photograph by David Schenk.

Also released in 1996, with John's participation, was a recorded tribute to Bill Monroe. Titled *True Life Blues*, the sampler honoring the Father of Bluegrass was produced by bassist Todd Phillips, issued by Sugar Hill Records, and included an all-star cast of musicians. In March 1995, John and Todd Phillips met up at Mark Howard's studio to commit "Little Cabin Home on the Hill," the Lester Flatt composition recorded by Bill with Lester and Earl Scruggs in 1947, to tape. Immediately, Todd disagreed with John's Hartfordesque approach to the song. John personalized "Cabin" by slowing the tempo, as well as utilizing chord substitutions, in stark contrast to the original. Therefore, when Todd rejected his arrangement, John ordered me to "pack up the instruments, we're leaving." I seem to remember being chased out into the street by Phillips, who negotiated with John to effect his return inside. On this occasion, unlike with the Civil War project,

John was serious about doing the song his way, as is obvious from the resulting recording.

Releasing two of his own albums, as well as participating in a third project for another producer, was typical of John's approach to his career. With no overarching plan, he'd often commit to multiple projects that competed with and, sometimes, dwarfed his own through larger budgets and better promotion.

At one of the few appearances I made backing John that year, reviewer Elizabeth Bruton wrote in the *Charlotte Observer* that, "Carlin is a phenomenal musician who fits extraordinarily well into the wonderful weirdness of this particular musical world." Her assessment continued:

> All four men [John Hartford, Mike Compton, Jerry McCoury, and Bob Carlin] improvise and follow, echoing each other, dueling string instruments—providing fun and entertainment for the audience and themselves. The improvisation keeps them fresh—in fact, the entire play list for any given performance is improvised on the spot, whatever Hartford feels like playing.
>
> You cannot get more real and alive than that.

STYLE CREATED BY LIMITATIONS

As I spent more and more time in Nashville working with John on various projects, I was often the recipient of John and Marie's hospitality. As a frequent guest in their Victorian house filled with steamboat architecture, I got to witness John's daily routines and work methods firsthand. This was an eye-opening experience, as I had never spent much time around any famous people, let alone someone as eccentric as John. John and Marie lived on the banks of the Cumberland River, to some degree, within a bubble of their own making.

Marie oversaw the household, as well as running the business of the record label and all that entailed. She sorted the mail, paid the bills, and supervised any work done to the residence and yard (eventually, residences, after they purchased the house next door). Marie's children were often employed to clean, do laundry, help her with the shopping and cooking, as well as any other of the myriad of small jobs required each day to, as John would say, "keep the boat in the channel."

Therefore, John's only task was to make music and earn the money necessary to support the Hartfords' lifestyle. He never had to mow the yard, wash his clothes, buy groceries, assemble a meal, or any of the other tasks necessary in overseeing a home. Reflecting on the situation from the present time, I believe (or at least it wouldn't have surprised me) that, for the entirety of his life, John *never* took on any of these responsibilities. When living at home, his mother primarily ran their residence. After he married, house management became the purview of his wives. In between those times, John covered some chores and hired out others. However, the day-to-day banalities were always predominantly carried out by the women in his life.

At the very least, I found the Hartfords' lifestyle foreign to me. In the middle-class world in which I lived, it was common for children to earn their allowance by doing chores such as collecting the household trash or yardwork. As an adult, I was partially responsible for every-thing that Marie, her staff, as well as John's accountant and booking agent, took on. I also split childcare responsibilities with my wife. John and Marie's lives seemed from my experience to be something of a fairytale existence detached from reality.

The whole situation appeared even more dysfunctional after I became a bigger part of John's music business. In the process, I gained a greater access to the workings of John and Marie's homestead. John often spoke about giving up some things to attain others, and his household was certainly a manifestation of that philosophy.

John's typical day at home began in the late morning or early after-noon. He would be seated at the long dining table with a panoramic view of the river completing the *New York Times* crossword puzzle (in pen!). After that, John spent lengthy periods there practicing his fiddle. On the table would be a recorder and a Dr. Beat Metronome he used to set tempos. John could sit for hours, obsessively trying phrases and tunes over and over, attempting to finesse his fiddle playing to the next level of excellence (John followed every idea *past* its logical conclusion). Although John liked to lend the appearance of spontane-ity to his performances, he was too much of a control freak to leave anything to chance. John was always well-rehearsed and warmed up; the spontaneity he championed would have to come from the other musicians in his ensembles. Every project was proceeded by a great deal of planning and the recording of a demo tape at his dining table.

John spent his musical life working at playing the banjo and the fiddle. His ultimate fiddle role model was Benny Martin and Earl Scruggs his goal on the banjo. After attempting to exactly mimic each of those musicians, he came to the realization in his early years as a professional entertainer that he would never meet their standards. Besides, even if he could approach the quality of their music, John would still only be an imitation of the original. From that point onward, John decided that he would develop his own personal approach, formulating distinctive fiddle and banjo methodologies.

On several occasions, John would attempt at verbalizing his distinctive approach to banjo and fiddle music. In the 1998 Smithsonian/PBS documentary and book *The Mississippi: River of Song*, John told the interviewer: "I think style is created by limitations. I do the very best I can with what I've got, and that's how it comes out. I would say that my life in music has been a steady thing of trying to teach my hands and my feet and my mouth to reproduce the sounds that I hear in my head."

The year before, in his album notes for *The Speed of the Old Long Bow*, John added, "I keep searching with my fingers for the sounds in my head and when I find more, I tend to want to erase everything I've done up to that moment, but I can't and such is the pain of the musician."

Finally, John told journalist Neil Strauss, "The reason that I'm in the business is because I love to play, and I love to explore where to go. What happens is you run up against a wall in your playing and you start searching along the wall and you find this door down here. And you open it up and there's this beautiful garden on the other side and you crawl through and all of a sudden, every tune that you know becomes a whole new experience again" ("Gentle Struggle for Perfection," New York Times News Service, *Minneapolis Star Tribune*, February 8, 2000).

During his lifetime, John produced multiple project ideas. Many of John's concepts and intentions never got past the planning or demo stage. In the time I knew him, these included a tribute to Roger Miller starring John and steel guitarist Buddy Emmons, a vocal duet album with singer Adie Grey, a fiddle album containing a catch-all collection of tunes, as well as, at the end of his life, a heavily Celtic-inspired recording of Hartford songs.

John was constantly recording his music to study it and (supposedly) evaluate it and improve it. He owned a succession of reel-to-reel tape recorders, which he used in the 1950s to capture the fiddlers from whom he wanted to learn as well as radio broadcasts of the musicians John emulated. In the 1960s and early 1970s, recordings documented song ideas and rehearsals. When John was in the Aereo-Plain band, he purchased an early monaural cassette recorder to evaluate their practices and jam sessions. As tape technology changed and became more affordable and portable, John embraced each upgrade and was an early adapter. When he passed, John's personal archive included years of recorded jam sessions, rehearsals, song and album ideas and source materials, as well as thousands of his live shows. (This collection is now housed at Middle Tennessee State University's Center For Popular Music.)

One downside I noticed to all of John's experimentation was that he often passed the point of rapidly diminishing returns. This applied to practicing the fiddle, where he once played every note slightly sharp for a week and, for the next, every note slightly flat. In his personal life, if consuming a half-gallon of water a day was good for you, multiple gallons had to be better. As a result, he washed all the electrolytes out of his body, triggering a bout of tachycardia.

John had a huge network of acquaintances scattered around the country, including visual artists, musicians, and riverboat enthusiasts. In the pre-internet days, John loved to spend hours speaking with his friends via telephone. His involvement with computers and the world wide web dated to the late 1990s, when he shifted his communications to email.

If John was at home in the evening, he liked to play Scrabble and was a ruthless, high-level competitor. Alternately, John was a fan of a range of movies. He also liked to attend area jam sessions, often playing with elite musicians such as the McCourys, the Osborne Brothers, and Earl Scruggs at the famous gatherings held by Larry Perkins.

When I was around and Marie was otherwise engaged, we'd often go out to eat in Madison at the Piccadilly Cafeteria. When journeying into Nashville proper, John and I would combine dining at Amerigo Italian restaurant or the Elliston Place Soda Shop with visits to Elder's, a high-end used book shop close by.

One time, in the Soda Shop, John related the story of a recent occasion when he had been in the establishment with bluegrass pioneer Bill Monroe. John had transported Bill to banjoist Rudy Lyle's funeral, stopping with Monroe for a meal following the service. When John returned to their table after paying the check, Bill Monroe was talking with their waitress. As John got within earshot, he caught the end of Monroe's conversation, which went: "You look like a girl who deserves a good spanking and I'm the one to give it to you, don't you know." For our repast, we happened to have that same waitress. When John asked her if she remembered the prior conversation with Bill, she replied: "I do believe he meant it!"

On other visits to downtown Nashville, John would enlist his best friend (and, eventually, the executor for his estate), instrument dealer George Gruhn, to eat sushi with us.

Although I don't remember John's poor behavior in restaurants when we were in the Nashville area, John admitted that he could be a difficult customer. John told of his younger days as a touring musician entering kitchens to yell at the chefs, and even when I traveled with John, he consistently gave restaurant staffs a hard time. This could be quite embarrassing for Hartford band members, some of whom chose to sit by themselves to avoid being associated with his actions. On the other hand, John was quite generous in choosing expensive restaurants and treating us to a meal of our choice. In the years of the second Hartford Stringband, rather than receive a per diem, John would just pay the full amount (within reason) for whatever you had spent on your meals.

John enjoyed these local forays away from the house behind the wheel of his Cadillac that had formerly belonged to banjoist Sonny Osborne. When we were in the midst of a recording project, John loved to do what he called "drive the album around" (that is, listen to the music over the car stereo). John was not alone in utilizing this method of evaluation, because it gives a different perspective to the music.

Besides eating, visiting with George Gruhn, or shopping for books and recordings, John would often take me along to call on his friends. When I had the time, I loved hanging out with John because, if I were patient, we'd go see somebody interesting or famous (or both), or someone interesting and/or famous would come to see him.

One time, we went to visit Jack Clement, who had produced three of John's recordings and introduced John to Mark Howard. Jack was in an expansive mood that day and generously allowed me to try out his rare personal early 1950s Gibson J-200 guitar (now housed at the Country Music Foundation), as well as a J-200-style ukulele made in his own shop. The Gibson had been utilized to pen many hit songs, and, throughout Jack's residency at Sun Records in Memphis and at his own studios in Nashville, the J-200 had graced countless important recordings.

These trips to shop, eat, and visit also occurred when we were traveling for engagements. Most of the time, John preferred to stay on the bus and work on his music. Occasionally, however, John would venture out with me to explore a bookshop, music store, or library.

One tour brought us to Philadelphia. There we ventured to the music retailer Vintage Instruments, where my former roommate, owner Fred Oster, broke out a Stradivarius violin. The instrument was destined for Christie's auction house in New York City, where Fred was also employed. John spent most of that day playing the Strad. We arrived in New York during the auction preview, and John had me accompany him to sample the violin once again.

When we left Christie's, John wanted to find a French restaurant with steak tartare. After a quick consult with the auction staff, we headed out to a small neighborhood brasserie. As we came through the door of the establishment, at a table sat the owner and the English guitar god Eric Clapton, who owned a residence in that part of the city. Thirty years before, Clapton's band Cream had appeared on both the original Smothers Brothers and Glen Campbell television programs, where John had met him.

On this particular day, I was a wise-ass and greeted Eric Clapton with "Look, John, its Eric Clapton." Clapton took one look at John, and then turned to the chef and made a right-hand finger-motion as if playing a banjo! Even after all those years, he remembered John and his music.

LAWRENCE HALEY LOVED "LOST INDIAN"

In 1997, John produced, recorded, and accompanied Gene Goforth, his longtime fiddling friend from Missouri, for a Rounder CD. Hartford also filmed his part for *The Mississippi: River of Song* and played banjo behind fiddler Jim Wood for *The Bullies Have All Gone to Rest*. John added to his Ed Haley tributes with the album *The Speed of the Old Long Bow*, which featured the flowering of the arranging method first attempted by John on his *Wild Hog* CD. Dubbed "windows," John describes this method in the album's notes:

> Everybody has a bunch of things they can do on their instruments—you can 1) play rhythm on the down beat, 2) play rhythm on the off-beat, 3) play a figure, like boogie woogie, 4) play a figure, like high or low bass runs, 5) play unison lead, 6) play harmony, 7) deaden your strings and play rhythm things, 8) play 4/4 chromatic runs, 9) play straight open chord rhythm, 10) play closed chords, 11) always play just one note like the tonic or 12) you can just lay out.
>
> So, every eight bars (a window), you change what you're doing or lay out (less is more). You might have five or six instruments and never more than three playing at the same time. The first window might be just the mandolin, the second window, just the banjo, the third, the mandolin doing something different and also adding the guitar. The next window might be everyone and then for contrast, just the fiddle. If it's a tune you haven't heard before you might want to listen for a window or two before you dive in. Or you can play something with anything the first time you hear it—even if it's one note or just something chromatic. An entrance or exit should sound on purpose and not fading in or out and we are trying to make each window real different from the one before.
>
> You can also lay out two windows (16 bars) if you need to, to change instruments or leave the stage for some reason like adjust the PA system, sell a tee shirt or kick somebody's posterior.
>
> The figure or lick does not have to be the same through the whole window as long as it works consistently as a window.

It's probably a good idea to lay out every third window any-way to keep it from getting too busy.

Generally, try and build with one, then two, then three instru-ments and then maybe, all of them and then lay out for pacing.

Additionally, John added into his album performances short spo-ken/sung couplets excerpted from his book-in-progress about Haley.

The first official attempt at a rehearsal by the album's core players was held in December 1996. Mike Compton (mandolin) and Dar-rin Vincent (guitar) from John's current touring group, along with myself on banjo, backed John's fiddling (Robert Gately was later added on bass).

John used this gathering to formally introduce his "new and improved" windows method. To further educate us, John had writ-ten out charts showing what each musician was to play based on the principles. We even tried several runs at the same tune after switch-ing charts between the different instruments. Ultimately, the version of the windows arranging method utilized for the album was less extreme than what was rehearsed, which was distilled even more for our later live performances.

At the rehearsal, sixteen of the tunes cut at the subsequent June recording session were attempted. (Between 1994 and 1997, fourteen of the cuts found on the Haley home recordings were played by John but ultimately left off from consideration for the CD). Another was added to rehearsals immediately preceding the sessions, with John undertaking an additional three fiddle tunes in the studio. Ultimately, fifteen of the pieces learned from Haley were issued.

Since John still wanted to record in Nashville, and Mark Howard, who owned John's studio of choice, disliked making fiddle albums, I recruited my first call engineer, Wes Lachot, to helm the sessions. By the way, Wes—a songwriter, musician, and highly acclaimed studio designer—loved working with John and participated in two subsequent John Hartford CDs. *The Speed of the Old Long Bow* was recorded on June 11 and 12, 1997, at Howard's Nashville studio.

After *The Speed of the Old Long Bow* was released in 1998, John only occasionally played the included Ed Haley tunes onstage. The exceptions were "(Three) Forks of Sandy," "Salt River" (which John

called "Push That Hogs Foot Further in the Bed" after the associated lyrics), and the medley of "Bonaparte's Retreat" / "Washington's
March," which he often preceded with "Dry and Dusty" rendered in
the same *scordatura* (altered) violin tuning.

As long as I had known John, he had been self-managed. With
input from Marie, accountant Bernie Saul, and booking agent Keith
Case, John managed to avoid the shoals and navigate to the open
waters of his career. Provided that there was a demand for John's services, this worked out successfully. When his pursuit of Ed Haley in
the 1990s coincided with a drop in his price and bookings, the expense
of touring began outpacing Hartford's concert income. Although it's
hard to say how much one led to or affected the other, it's a fact
that John's output of vocal albums diminished in the second half of
the decade. It's possible that, by becoming too self-absorbed with his
musical passions, he had helped to hasten this professional decline.

On a trip to New York City, which I believe occurred in 1997 or
1998, John and I left the drivers and other musicians sleeping on the
bus and went to eat breakfast. He surprised me by bringing up his
discontent with the downward course of his career and his management situation. John had become concerned about the organizational
strategy. He suggested that I take on a management role, to coordinate
between all the various entities. Additionally, I was to formulate a
plan to improve the number of his engagements and increase his fees.

Unfortunately, this proved to be too radical a proposal for those
involved. John got cold feet about the changes and tensions that this
would involve. When his cancer reemerged, the idea was never again
considered.

In 1997, as in previous years, I appeared as a member of John's
backup band on recordings. For a few occasions, around recording
sessions with John or at concerts near my North Carolina home, I was
also called upon to join the John Hartford band on stage. However, at
the end of 1997, events would cause a dramatic change in John's act. By
1998, a whole different approach and sound would draw me full-time
into the John Hartford Stringband.

CHAPTER FOUR

I COULD ALWAYS DO THIS SHOW WITHOUT YOU

This would be a sad old world
Without a lot of good old boys
—"GOOD OLD BOYS"

John began 1998 at the peak of his musical powers. He then set about finding and integrating a group of players—the instrumental combination of guitar, mandolin, banjo, and bass John had been utilizing for his recordings—into a collective unit that could handle anything he threw at them. This encompassed his stage repertoire of fiddle tunes, original and traditional songs, as well as any new material John might conjure up. However, this would take time to develop, and the first part of 1998 was filled with growing pains for the newly gathered ensemble.

Before the formation of the group, John's band personnel would vary wildly for low-key gigs like the Museum of Appalachia, as well as local Nashville appearances at the Station Inn and the yearly benefit concerts for Keith McReynolds. Even away from home, depending on who was available, John might perform solo or in any variety of instrumental combinations. Some of this variety was influenced by, rather than keeping a group on salary, John's attempt at saving money thru paying by the tour. As he once told us, "I could always do this show without you." However, once the Hartford Stringband solidified into the quartet that made John's final recordings, this combination of musicians was what he favored.

The real beginnings for the live iteration of Hartford Stringband version two, the successor to the triple fiddle group of the late 1980s,

John Hartford and the Hartford Stringband, April 24–26, 1998, MerleFest, Wilkesboro, NC. L to r: Bob Carlin, Mike Compton, John Hartford, Mark Schatz, Chris Sharp. The first "official" appearances for the full band that recorded *Good Old Boys*. Notice we are using microphones for each instrument. Collection of the author.

occurred with the hiring of guitarist Chris Sharp. Larry Christopher Sharp (born 1973) had been invited by John to the 1997 Tennessee Fall Homecoming, where the format allowed John to experiment onstage with different combinations of instrumentalists.

Raised outside Asheville in the Western North Carolina mountains, Sharp came from a musical family. Chris moved to the Nashville area for his employment by John and was to accompany him for the remainder of John's life.

Chris vividly recalls that, after arriving in Norris (probably on Saturday evening before the festival's final day), he located John at the Golden Girls restaurant jam session. Upon playing just one song with him, John told Chris, "That's the sound I've been searching for," and hired him on the spot. John had discovered and hired a guitarist who could anchor any ensemble of musicians he chose to fulfill his musical vision.

Chris joined regular John Hartford mandolinist Mike Compton, bassist Mark Schatz (replacing the recently deceased Roy Huskey Jr.), and Larry Perkins on banjo for John's last day of performances at the

Homecoming. The classically trained Schatz (born 1955) had a long history in various bluegrass groups, from Tasty Licks and Spectrum with banjoist Bela Fleck, groundbreaking guitarist Tony Rice's Unit, as well as hit songwriter Tim O'Brien's O'Boys. Born in Indiana, Larry Perkins was a good friend of John's and a key member of the Nashville bluegrass community. Besides Hartford standbys "Love Grown Cold" and "Gentle on My Mind," those sets featured a variety of fiddle melodies off John's two Rounder CDs highlighting the music of Ed Haley.

As John was to later write in the liner notes to Sharp's first CD, "When Chris is combined with Mike Compton, our favorite mandolin player . . . , they make up our favorite rhythm section." For all intents and purposes, this was the origin point for the last Hartford Stringband.

After a five-month break from performing with John, I arrived for his appearance at the Down Home, a small venue in Johnson City, Tennessee. The band for the evening of February 7, 1998, besides several guest performers, was just Chris and me. Our first meeting was a bit rocky, as neither of us had been informed by John about the other. Many months later, after he had, in Johnspeak, "gotten used" to my personality, Chris told me that he had never been around anyone like me before. Chris had come up playing bluegrass music with other southerners. I had been raised outside New York City and had the directness and sense of humor common to northerners. This was not a recipe for instant rapport!

It took some time for the new lineup to stabilize. Based on availability, John's shows over the next several months drew various combinations of musicians from the core of Mike Compton (mandolin), Chris Sharp (guitar), Mark Schatz (bass), and myself (banjo). Besides gigs in the Nashville area, Mike, Chris, and I traveled with John to his "other hometown" of St. Louis. There we appeared on February 21 at the Calvin Opera House in Washington, Missouri, just west of the city. At the end of March, Chris and Mark journeyed to Michigan for John's concerts. The John Hartford trio played a show benefiting Kentuckians for the Commonwealth before heading to MerleFest for the first appearance by the full band. From that point on, the Stringband—with Mark Schatz or Larry Perkins on bass—exclusively backed John.

One thing that needed integration by all of us was the adaptation to the variety of material we were required to perform. These were challenging but exciting times for the Hartford band. Mike and Chris had come out of bluegrass music—Chris scrutinizing Lester Flatt–style rhythm guitar and Mike studying the subtleties of mandolinist Bill Monroe. Although I had a knowledge of bluegrass and popular music, my banjo style was based on backing fiddle tunes. It was a leap of faith for John to throw an old time-style banjoist into the middle of a bluegrass ensemble, and a challenge for both me and the bluegrassers to tackle the complex chord changes utilized for some of John's songs.

Before his final bout of illness, we never knew what John was going to play onstage. Outside of "Gentle on My Mind," John would often pull out obscure songs from his or bluegrass music's past that none of us knew, let alone had ever played.

Ultimately, we all changed our approaches to suit John's requirements. The results were nothing short of groundbreaking, albeit in a way very similar, but subtler and less influential, to the Aereo-Plain band.

As with many things in John's life, he modeled his style of band leadership on his heroes such as Bill Monroe. John, therefore, gave little musical direction outside of, "I'm going to do my solo show and all of you figure out something to do behind it." The most instruction from John, mimicking Monroe's onstage behavior, was to stand behind you and chop rhythm to communicate tempo changes, turn around and say, "Key of D," or, to tell you, "Don't do that again" after a solo or an antic of which he didn't approve. On the positive side, with the freedom John gave us within his music, both Mike Compton and I came up with new approaches for playing our instruments. Because I couldn't initially visualize banjo parts for all of John's core repertoire, for the pieces of John's that required it, I switched to rhythm guitar. It took me the better part of six months to entirely integrate my banjo playing into the Stringband.

John was nothing if not eccentric, and I suppose that raised his tolerance for excessive behavior within our group of misfits. In all the time that I knew him, I never heard of his firing anyone. The closest he ever came to dismissing a member of his band was when John suggested that person "take a break for a while." Whenever Chris, Mike,

Larry, or I acted up or behaved badly, John's strongest reprimand was, "Well, I guess you shouldn't do that again."

However, John also had a temper, as well as a long-term desire to be at the center and in control of every situation. On a few occasions, when John felt threatened, he could withhold onstage features, or deny one of us access to career opportunities. Additionally, John enjoyed setting up situations that pitted band members against each other or manipulated an individual. For example, John liked to torment guitarist Chris Sharp by playing what musicians characterize as "behind the beat" almost to the point of dragging. As a result, Chris would struggle to keep our performance rhythmically moving forward.

John's tolerance contrasted sharply with the way most other groups were run. After John's death, I was on a trial basis with another band when the leader made a comment on stage about not paying me because I was a wealthy Jew and didn't need the money. At intermission, I made my case offstage about that stereotype being offensive and requested that it be deleted from the show. The bandleader apologized. But I wasn't asked to become a permanent band member after that night. My personality is too strong to exist within most normal musical aggregations.

As much as he required a backup band of high-quality musicians to inspire him, John was also looking for (when he wanted) interesting companions who shared his interests. The Stringband was as much his "posse" (in the modern parlance) as his employees.

For that first year of the Hartford Stringband, as the gigs had been booked and advertised as "John Hartford" without mentioning a band, both promoters and audiences were surprised and puzzled upon our arrival. In their defense, I don't think it was John's original intention to form an ensemble that would share equal stage time with him. After all, it was his name on the marquee and his show and agent and bus that got us all to and from the concerts. We had been hired by John because he wanted us to be a part of his music. Consequently, without support from his booking agent or the promoters (after all, they worked for John, not the band members), we were mostly ignored by his audiences. However, once the *Good Old Boys* album was released and we started to appear more consistently onstage with John, listeners came to expect and welcome the Hartford Stringband.

L to r: Mike Compton, Bob Carlin, John Hartford, Mike Bub, Chris Sharp. July 18, 1998, Mid-West National Bluegrass Festival, Lima, OH. Three months after MerleFest and we've made the switch to a single microphone onstage. John had been intrigued by the traditional stage choreography possible around a solo mic setup.

With MerleFest at the end of April kicking off spring and summer touring for 1998, John and the Stringband played their first extended run of engagements. Because John had decided some years before to give up "routing dates" (that is, appearances with a low monetary guarantee taken to fill in between better paying gigs), John and the Stringband often traveled long distances by bus, van, or airplane to stand-alone engagements. These included, in June, the Mystic, Connecticut, Seaport; Twenty-Fifth Annual Bluegrass Festival in Telluride, Colorado; and the Kentucky Folk Festival/KETV taping; in July, Ohio's Mid-West National Bluegrass Festival and (the city of) Hartford, Connecticut's Mark Twain Days; and August's Bean Blossom Jam Fest in Indiana and the Lake County Folk Festival in Illinois.

A large proportion of John's engagements resulted from his association with river travel. I dubbed his ten-day August sojourn to the upper Midwest "The Water Tour" because the contracted venues all sat on lakes or rivers. We shared a number of shows with other bands and, because Mike Compton had stayed at home to await the birth of his first child and Mark Schatz was otherwise engaged, we often borrowed musicians from those groups. Therefore, Gene Libbea of the Nashville Bluegrass Band and Mike Bub of Del McCoury's group were our bassists, and mandolin duties for two gigs were handled by Ronnie McCoury. For the penultimate concert, we provided the entertainment aboard the *Julia Belle Swain*, where John had been a crew member. The occasion was the retirement party for *Waterways Journal* editor Jimmy Swift.

Midway through summer touring, two changes occurred in John's appearances. For one, he switched to a single microphone on stage. Citing the influence of Del McCoury, John had been intrigued by the traditional stage choreography possible around a solo mic setup. Additionally, it theoretically simplified staging and shortened the time needed for preshow arrangements. Finally, it took away much of the control of the mix from the sound person and gave it back to the musicians.

The second adjustment was my assuming responsibility for selling merchandise at engagements. As noted, when I first met John, merch sales had been handled by Marie. His wife enjoyed the interactions with John's audiences, and often became friendly with his fans. She used these interchanges to determine what John Hartford followers would buy and, therefore, what items to manufacture and keep in stock. When not purchasing merchandise such as recordings from John's back catalogue, Marie would determine and have an input into releases on Small Dog.

Before I began touring full-time with John, Marie sold a greater variety of items, including T-shirts designed by John. Commissioned by the couple, the garments showcased his characteristic florid script handwriting reproduced along with historic photographs and, on some occasions, one of John's line drawings. Probably Marie's most famous product, which gained some traction, were her John Hartford teddy bears. These stuffed animals were dressed in John's stage outfit, sporting a replica derby, vest, and banjo in miniature.

Sometime after the middle of 1995, familial responsibilities mandated that Marie spend more time at home. Additionally, I got the impression that the bus had become too crowded for her liking once John filled the vehicle with three to four other male musicians.

With Marie absent, John assigned the responsibilities for merchandise sales to the lead bus drivers, often with mixed results. That meant, with the formation of the John Hartford Stringband in 1998, merch was being handled by Jimmy Johnson. However, unlike Marie, Jimmy was never fully committed to selling CDs, T-shirts, and the like. Sometimes his other duties would draw him away from sales and keeping the inventory and organization of the merchandise bay under the bus up to date. What resulted was a lack of many titles from John's recorded catalogue with the subsequent missed retailing opportunities. John didn't improve things by often helping himself to recordings and shirts, giving them away, or stashing boxes in his home office. Jimmy was therefore happy to hand me the responsibility for sales and I was able to have a positive effect on the income from John's product.

Unfortunately, by the time I took over, Marie had lost interest in stocking John's merchandise and in the generation of new items. Therefore, the T-shirts and teddy bears had been discontinued. Additionally, Marie was resistant to purchasing copies of John Hartford CDs from other labels such as Rounder, which issued the majority of John's output in the 1990s. And Small Dog's output had slowed to a trickle, so, there were fewer new titles from the company as well.

Marie would have preferred selling off the large overstock of *Old Sport* and *Cadillac Rag*. Unfortunately, John's fans either wanted his latest output, the "classics" like *Aereo-Plain*, or "greatest hits" collections such as *Live at College Station*.

Therefore, in addition to begging Marie to pay Rounder and other record labels to be able to order more copies of their releases, I would often scour the house for various hidden items. These included posters, 8 × 10" promotional photographs, 45 rpm records, cassettes, and LPs, the last of which, by the late 1990s, had gone out of fashion (however, they made great platforms for John's signature!). Therefore, fully stocked with those additional pieces, it wasn't uncommon to gross thousands of dollars in merchandise sales at each performance.

Now, here's to all them good old boys
Cheer 'em on, make a lot of noise
—"Good Old Boys"

At MerleFest 1998, John and I had met with Happy Traum of Homespun Tapes. We negotiated for John to provide his services to Homespun for two videos of instructional material. Titled *The Banjo According to John Hartford*, Happy scheduled a shoot in Nashville for mid-July. I was to coordinate the production, with Chris Sharp accompanying John on guitar and fiddle. If you want to really understand John's approach to learning music and his practice regiment, this video set, along with the fiddle instructional John made for *Fiddler* magazine (*John Hartford's Old Time Fiddling: "Trying to teach my hands to do what I hear in my head"*), are essential viewing.

Early on in his musical journey, John had figured out that he would need to invent something original to really stand out and make his mark. After spending his formative years imitating Earl Scruggs on the banjo, he came up with several unique approaches that John explains within these instructional DVDs. He was to utilize this reworked method for much of his post-Hollywood career.

One is what he called the "pull-off style." It is exactly as described: instead of plucking with his right hand each individually fingered left-hand note, John starts a musical series with a right-hand pluck and then "pulls off" (plucks with his left hand) the remaining sequence of pitches.

Another technique that helps to define the Hartford banjo style involves what John dubbed his "slide whistle chord." This fingering allows John to slide a dissonant, partially chromatic run across successive strings up and down the fingerboard.

Both techniques—the pull-off style and slide whistle chord—are often coupled by John with dropped or "ghost" notes. The resulting "missing notes" in his melodic passages aid John's playing at breakneck tempos. That is, when he isn't playing stripped-down melodies at beautifully slow speeds!

Within these instructional recordings, John explains his very thorough approach to the banjo, including hand position, tone production, phrasing, accents, and working with a metronome. John teaches some of his most famous songs utilizing banjo accompaniment and relates a few stories about his history of making music. My favorite tale involves a visit to Earl Scruggs's home to play banjos together. John went way beyond obsession when trying different approaches to improve his playing, often tweaking the smallest aspects of his technique. To upgrade his tone, John had filed his finger picks into sharp points. At Earl's, with Scruggs picking his low-grade at-home instrument complete with a torn head, John recorded the playing of the two men. Later, when listening back to the tape, John was floored that his banjo sounded tinny and weak while Scruggs's inexpensive instrument sounded full and strong. It was a good lesson for John that sound is in the picking hand of the individual, not in the picks or instrument.

The Banjo According to John Hartford sessions were not without their problems. John decided (erroneously) that, instead of a lavalier microphone clipped onto his shirt, a microphone on a stand would more closely attain his artistic goals. It didn't matter that this compromised the sound quality and negatively impacted the look of the video. To maintain control of the taping, John asserted his star power to bend Traum and the crew to his will. The bigger issue had nothing to do with John and occurred at a later editing session. An engineering mistake caused some of the footage to be erased, which required my spending extra time reworking the surviving material into a finished product.

During a second break from touring, two albums featuring John and the Hartford Stringband members emerged. In early September 1998, John honored his promise to Chris Sharp by helping arrange and performing on Sharp's solo recording for Red Clay Records (whose name John in an unconscious homage to Steve Goodman's Red Pajamas Records would often purposely mangle as something like the "Red Underwear label" or "Red Flannel Pajama label"). Titled *Good Fa-air Side* ("Good for Our Side" in John- and Chris-speak), onstage John once announced Sharp's album title as *Foggy Marlon Brando*, a play on Earl Scruggs's *Foggy Mountain Banjo* album. John also labeled the group that recorded it as "Flatt & Sharp" or "Hat & Sharp." This was a multiple word-play exercise on Flatt & Scruggs substituting Chris's last name for Earl's as well as that the music contained/or can either be flat or sharp (and that Lester and Earl and Chris all wore hats onstage).

Sharp's CD was waxed at Jack Clement's Studio, where John had worked on his five recordings made between 1984 and 1992. The sessions also featured Stringband member Mike Compton and future members Larry Perkins on banjo and Matt Combs on fiddle.

Besides adding fiddle, banjo, and harmony vocals, John contributed "Love Grown Cold," included on the *Hartford & Hartford* release (written by Johnny Bond), as well as his own compositions "Here I Am in Love Again" (from 1989's *Down on the River*) and the only officially released recording of John's original banjo instrumental "Foggy Mountain Landscape." The title is obviously an homage to the Earl Scruggs standard "Foggy Mountain Breakdown," and John felt compelled to get Earl's permission before naming this banjo instrumental. (Aside from the use of tuners like those debuted by Scruggs, "Landscape" bears no discernible relationship to "Breakdown.")

John began utilizing elements of "The Landscape," as John often referred to his tune, onstage as early as the middle of 1994. The ideas were shelved until John dusted off a more complete, but still embryonic, version of this piece for Chris. This prompted Sharp's encouragement for John to develop more fully the instrumental. It's possible the composition was also influenced by a set of "Scruggs tuners" crafted and gifted to John at MerleFest 1998 by his longtime friend Henry Lewis.

From early 1998 through the beginning of 1999, John continued to reshape and reformulate "Foggy Mountain Landscape" in front of audiences, even after the sessions for Sharp's CD had concluded. John featured "The Landscape" in the slot showcasing his banjo playing during shows through the end of 2000, when he was forced by his deteriorating health to abandon the instrument.

Twenty-five years later, I'm puzzled by John's gift of his unrecorded instrumental "Foggy Mountain Landscape" to Sharp's album. Since John was about to record his own disc, why wouldn't he have saved "The Landscape"? It would have made a wonderful addition to *Good Old Boys*.

One reason might have been that, according to Chris Sharp, "Foggy Mountain Landscape" became fully developed because Chris encouraged John's original idea. Another explanation is that true to form, John wasn't thinking about his own career when committing "The Landscape" to Chris Sharp's CD.

Poster, J. D'Addario & Company, ca. 1998. John Hartford and the Hartford Stringband, l to r: Mark Schatz, Chris Sharp, John Hartford, Bob Carlin, Mike Compton. This promotional poster utilizes Jim Dirden's photograph made at MerleFest and featured on the cover of *Good Old Boys*. Photograph by Jim Dirden. Collection of the author.

Although I don't begrudge Chris, and it was in character for John to compete with his own release, I still find this behavior perplexing.

Almost immediately upon the conclusion of recording with Sharp at Jack Clement's, the band adjourned to Durham, North Carolina, with the goal being laying down the tracks slated for the next CD under the John Hartford name. Besides the Hartford Stringband—Compton, Sharp, Carlin, and Schatz—along for these September sessions at Overdub Lane was banjoist Larry Perkins. Rather than focus on fiddle instrumentals, this album was to be a showcase for a new set of John's original songs.

The plan was to record quickly and mostly live, with the only later additions being harmony vocals. The arrangements as such, without much rehearsal in advance or in the studio, emerged as they were cut. Most of the songs were captured in only one or two takes. John had decided to add to the spontaneity by starting performances while the band was still tuning. John liked to create situations (musical and otherwise) that knocked other people off balance to see how they'd react and recover, and what they'd create. The resulting album therefore has the band jumping in during the first few bars of each selection.

Four of the issued songs received extensive rehearsals in front of an audience in advance of the sessions. These included the title tune, "Good Old Boys." It was originally published in 1971 as a part of John's book of lyrics and poems *Word Movies* under the title "Them Good Old Boys." John was very proud that the disc jockey and syndicated radio personality Wolfman Jack (aka Robert Weston Smith) used to quote the poem on his late-night radio program.

John had been performing "Good Old Boys" onstage for two months. After the album's release, John utilized the song's chorus and structure as a performance vehicle for introducing the Stringband's members.

"Keep on Truckin'" was another song from the early 1970s. Before inclusion on *Good Old Boys*, it was recorded with different verses for John's *Aereo-Plain* record, ultimately going unused.

The origins for "The Waltz of the Golden Rule" date to at least spring 1993, when John began using a part of its lyrics as a spoken outro to his performances ("The old bald spot on top of the head"). The musical version, with its recorded but unissued double-time coda, was performed all thorough the month leading up to the sessions for *Good Old Boys* but never again after that time. John *did* choose, however, to end post-session sets on occasion with the original spoken admonition to "Go home, get into bed, and do unto others as you would have them do unto you."

The centerpiece for the *Good Old Boys* collection was the ten-minutes-plus tribute to his musical hero Bill Monroe. Titled "The Cross-Eyed Child," within the lyrics and spoken sections of this composition, John poetically talks about his interactions with Monroe. John's relating of Bill's life story highlighted Monroe's youth, which was partially spent neglected and mocked because of his poor vision, and how it shaped his later life. Among all the newly written pieces, John had spent the most time reworking and refining "The Cross-Eyed Child." It obviously had strong meaning for him.

John had begun introducing "The Cross-Eyed Child" into his sets by 1996. He experimented on stage for two and half years with tempos, time signatures, lyrics, as well as other aspects of the structure and arrangement. John often followed this song onstage with one of Monroe's original instrumental mandolin tunes. Led by Mike Compton, this was usually either "Wheel Hoss" or "Roanoke." I believe an earlier studio version by John recorded by Mark Howard remains unreleased. "The Cross-Eyed Child" stayed a staple of John's repertoire through the live "Tribute to John Hartford" in 2000 recorded at Nashville's War Memorial Auditorium for the *Mountain Stage* radio program.

Played for the first time during these recordings, the bit of whimsy titled "Watching the River Go By" was frequently performed afterward by John. By the spring of 2000, he had switched from sung to rambling spoken verses. John last played this song at his penultimate show in April 2001.

"On the Radio" outlined John's teenage search for bluegrass music over the airwaves. The song was heard on stage as early as January 1997 and performed after the sessions leading up to the release of the CD.

Many of the other Hartford originals published on this album, including "The Waltz of the Mississippi," "Dixie Trucker's Home," "Owl Feather," "Mike & John in the Wilderness," and "Billy the Kid," either were never performed or were featured on stage only once or twice in John's sets.

Album outtakes included several songs and tunes drawn from traditional music, including "Old Cow Died." That was mostly performed leading up to the September sessions, and a live version from the June 1998 event in Telluride, Colorado, was issued on a festival CD.

Two other songs written by John were attempted but not included in the final album order. "I Don't Need Work, I Need Money," cowritten with Mark Schatz, was based on an offhand comment. Jamie Harford, I'm assuming many years before, had approached John for some financial help. John offered his son employment working around his home, and this was Jamie's reply. The song, with an improvised spoken middle section by myself, was first performed in January 1998 and played live numerous times before the August sessions. "Yes, We Will Gather Round the TV" was claimed by John to have been written a month before it was recorded. However, live tapes indicate that the band had already learned it by that time.

Good Old Boys broke with John's blueprint of new songs, rerecordings, and standards for a new album. Although compositions from other resources were tracked, the released album contained only John's own material. Covers from his own prior records and chestnuts documented in the studio were excluded from the final order.

As I witnessed John's songwriting process and listened more intently to all his recorded catalogue, I became aware that he wrote at least three types of songs. Some were just thrown off, composed quickly with a memorable chorus, as a structure for soloing. One example from *Good Old Boys* would be "Keep on Truckin'." For others, John focused more time and energy on the melody and the lyrical structure and story. Songs in this grouping showed John's influence from the seemingly nonsensical prose of writers such as Lewis Carroll and Ogden Nash. An illustration would be "Owl Weather." The last category included those "story songs" that required major investments of time and thought. These were crafted lyrics and represented miniature short narratives about specific subjects or people. An example from *Good Old Boys* is "On the Radio."

It's hard to say, after the fact, how much I, as the producer, like David Bromberg almost thirty years before, influenced the selection and shaping of *Good Old Boys*. It's possible, like Bromberg, that I called for the collection to focus on John Hartford originals. To the best of my recollection, John and I collaborated on choosing the eleven tracks that were the most fully realized and the most successful in representing him as a songwriter.

Both Chris Sharp's *Good "Fa-air" Side* and *Good Old Boys* were released in 1999.

John had methods, theories, and formulas that applied to the entirety of his day-to-day life. These were utilized for everything from brushing his teeth to how he changed strings on his instruments to songwriting. Although these systems would change from time to time (therefore the maxim of "I do something 110 percent until I decide to do something else"), there were always rules to govern all aspects of John's schedule.

While I was performing with John, he tried to get all of us to practice songwriting. Mike Compton was already composing mandolin instrumentals, Chris Sharp wanted to try writing, and Mark Schatz coauthored with John on occasion. I was the only holdout. The reasons I gave were, one, I thought there were already enough good (and bad) songs in the world without my mediocre attempts. And two, it was intimidating to write in front of a master like John Hartford. So I resisted John's advances until after his passing.

This didn't curtail John's continued encouragement. One suggestion that he put forward was to take an existing song or fiddle instrumental (John felt traditional fiddle tunes, because they had survived over time, must contain the greatest melodies), write new lyrics, and then change the melody. John utilized this method on several occasions for songs such as "The Julia Belle Swain" (the result a mash-up of Stephen Foster's steamboat anthem "The Glendy Burk" and the fiddle tune "Over the Waterfall") as well as "I Wish We Had Our Time Again" (utilizing a similarly named fiddle tune). Of course, John never wrote new melodies for either song.

John was constantly writing down ideas for new compositions on his 3-by-5 cards. If something occurred that he thought would work well as a lyrical idea, he'd note it down. When one of us said something interesting, John would often ask for permission to use the phrase and annotate it on a card. As an illustration of that practice, he told an apocryphal but emblematic story about Harlan Howard. Like many Nashville songwriters of the time, Harlan was signed to a publishing deal that gave him a salary advance against future royalties, described in the business as a "draw." Alone or with other song crafters, he would write for part of the day, collect his draw, and then go to a hangout and drink with other tunesmiths. One day, a "new guy" was at the other end of the bar talking to the bartender, who was asking him why he looked so downtrodden. "I don't know," he replied, "I guess tonight, the bottle let me down." All the songwriters in the room looked at each other, and then made a mad dash to get back to their offices and craft a song based on that line. (The song "The Bottle Let Me Down" was actually written and recorded by Merle Haggard, not Harlan Howard. But the story still contains an element of truth.)

For some of John's creations, the idea that triggered the song or the inspiration for a line or image is fairly obvious to me. Having known him for fifteen years and witnessed his songwriting process, as well as my long-term study of his music, revealed much about these influences. John constantly referenced source material from bluegrass and traditional music, name-checked family, musicians, and friends in the steamboat community, and weaved observed incidents into his lyrics.

Engineer Wes Lachot, himself a serious writer of songs, was impressed when, during the *Good Old Boys* sessions, John emerged from the restroom with three new ones. "And a few were pretty good," Wes later remarked.

Immediately following the sessions, it was back on the road for John and the Stringband. Along for the ride was Larry Perkins, replacing Mark Schatz on bass and occasional banjo.

John's group made a swing through New England and New York from September 18 to 26. We followed with a pair of gigs in New Jersey and Mobile, Alabama, on October 3 and 4. John's yearly pilgrimage to the Tennessee Fall Homecoming, along with November's trip to St. Louis, were made without me. After eating a Thanksgiving meal at the Hartford residence, John, the band, and I spent the last weekend of November in the upper Midwest.

First I play one of theirs.

Not surprisingly, John's large performing repertoire with the Hartford Stringband drew from his twenty song-centric albums recorded over as many years, along with his lifelong study of music from a variety of genres. In 1998, about twenty songs were played live only once. Of those, four were requests and an additional two served as encores. Seven came from the 1970s, four from the 1980s, and six from John's albums of the 1990s.

From his earliest days performing solo in the 1970s, John had utilized multiple instruments to create variety onstage. Usually starting with the fiddle, John would rotate to the banjo and guitar at least several times a night. Multiple pieces were played on each instrument before going on to the next.

John used to describe his approach to structuring a set as: "First I play one of theirs [what the audience came to hear]. If that works, I play another one of theirs. Then, I play one of ours [one the audience wants to hear that John also would choose to perform]. And, if the audience is still with me, I'll play one of mine [an obscure selection that the fans wouldn't have heard before]."

When John convened the Hartford Stringband, he was still following the above strictures and philosophy. A notable "one of theirs" that we always played was John's biggest hit song, "Gentle on My Mind," which would often lead off his concerts. It goes without saying that he had been playing "Gentle" at every performance since he and I had met. However, around 1990, John began moving away from the banjo approach utilized on the original recording. Instead, he went with a fiddle arrangement which substituted a simpler three-chord structure (as recorded on *No End of Love* and released in 1996) for the original more complex progression.

Always in the number two slot of his concerts was an original blues that John had recorded in 1989. Performed since its release, "Bring Your Clothes Back Home" provided a good showcase for solos from the Stringband members. Another song featuring the fiddle was "More Bull Fiddle Fun." Included on *The Walls We Bounce Off Of*, "Bull Fiddle Fun" was often sung to whatever melody John happened to be playing at the time. "Love Grown Cold" from Johnny Bond, featured on the *Hartford & Hartford* CD, was equally presented on the banjo and the fiddle.

The banjo portions of John's programs usually employed the songs "Gum Tree Canoe," an S. S. Steele composition; "Way Down the River Road," one of his own compositions that drew from musical traditions; and "Lorena," another Hartford arrangement. All were recorded for John's 1984 album *Gum Tree Canoe*. A fourth banjo feature, "Steam Powered Aereo Plane," dated to the *Aereo-Plain* album of 1971.

The guitar portion of the show leaned on "In Tall Buildings." Originally written and recorded for his unreleased final RCA album *Radio John*, John's song was recast and issued in 1980 on *Nobody Knows What You Do*. The story of the transition from youthful pursuits to adult responsibilities ("They'll sell me a suit, they'll cut off my hair, and send me to work in tall buildings"), it was another that John featured for the fifteen years we were acquainted.

"One of theirs" and "one of ours" could have applied to the various songs that were rotated through our sets in 1998. Fiddle-led compositions included "Skippin' in the Mississippi Dew" (recorded in 1970 and 1976), "Long Hot Summer Day" (1976), "Miss Ferris" (1978), "Annual Waltz" (1987), "M.I.S.I.P." (1992), and the mysterious "The Rest Is Up to You" (1998). Joining "In Tall Buildings" on guitar was 1967's "Washing Machine." There was a long list of banjo songs spanning John's career: "Boogie" (which John once called "Probably the worst song I wrote in my life"), "Cripple Creek," "The Girl I Left Behind Me," "Goin' Back to Dixie," "Here I Am in Love Again," "I Wonder Where You Are Tonight," "The Julia Belle Swain," "The Mississippi Queen," and "Short Life of Trouble."

The "one[s] of mine," which grew more numerous at the end of 1990s, covered a variety of fiddle tunes occasionally thrown into John's sets. The ones that were played on multiple occasions included two tunes John utilized for his square dance encores and two standards that were part of his stage sets as long as I had known John. This grouping included the warhorse "Orange Blossom Special." Six of those performed on multiple occasions were recorded for John's all instrumental Rounder albums of the mid-1990s. The most-performed example of this second collection was "The Squirrel Hunters" from *Wild Hog in the Red Brush*. The last—"Golden Eagle Hornpipe"—John had begun playing in the 1990s. This "book" tune was probably learned by John because it was named for a steamboat.

The only limits John placed on his repertoire appeared to be a few of the songs from his hippie days of the 1970s. On several occasions, John indicated to me that these counterculture set pieces embarrassed him and wouldn't be well received by his current audience.

Two examples were "The Golden Globe Awards" and "Smoke, Shit and F**k." "Golden Globe" was originally featured on 1976's *Nobody Knows What You Do*. This tribute to the ample breasts of a lover, was once requested by a couple on their anniversary and reluctantly performed by John at a concert. "Smoke" had been a crowd pleaser at large "gatherings of the tribes" in the 1970s and 1980s. When I requested that Rounder include a demo of "Smoke" from the 1970s on a CD of *Aereo-Plain* outtakes, John insisted that it be excluded.

As 1998 concluded, things looked bright for 1999. John's first album featuring the Stringband would be released, and the improvements shown in 1998 could only continue in the new year. Unfortunately, while the end of the decade offered new opportunities for John, the coming millennium also brought back a formidable adversary.

Chapter Five

You Certainly Are Easily Entertained, and for That, I Am Eternally Grateful

Out behind the firehouse, under a full moon
Fiddlers and banjo pickers, crammed inside a room
Playing songs that were popular, back in 1943
Raising the roof, in a little white house
In Madison, Tennessee
—"Madison Tennessee"

In 1999, as John continued his touring backed by the Hartford String-band, the two albums recorded in 1998 appeared. Featuring the members of John's stage ensemble, *Good Old Boys* and Chris Sharp's solo album *Good Fa'Air Side* debuted about the same time in October. Along with the two CDs, John's banjo instructional videos for Home-spun, *The Banjo According to John Hartford*, also emerged that year. John's collaboration with David Grisman and Mike Seeger, titled *Retrograss*, additionally was released on Grisman's label, Acoustic Disc. That trio performed seven concerts in 2000. Finally, *The Mississippi: River of Song* multimedia project debuted. Spearheaded by the Smithsonian Institution, John was featured in this series documenting modern life on the Mississippi River. Rather than worry about diluting his brand or competing with his own projects, John was determined to keep busy while he still could function.

As the occasions increased where promoters didn't expect a full band, we didn't know exactly where we were headed, or we remained unaware of details such as complimentary hotel rooms, I decided to take matters into my own hands as de facto road manager. Beginning with appearances where we flew and expanding to all other engagements, I started either calling John's booking agency or going into the office to gather details for John's upcoming gigs. Furthermore, I kept track of set lengths and served as John's "right hand" onstage. Fortunately, I was used to controlling these aspects both within my own touring as well as through prior work with artists such as Scottish guitarist Bert Jansch and Black fiddler Joe Thompson.

With Chris Sharp the designated band leader, Mike Compton in charge of stage setup, and Mike and Larry Perkins piloting the tour bus, all bases were covered within the members of the group.

By the middle of 1999, the Hartford Stringband began hitting its stride. The accumulation of onstage experience, along with the addition of the arrangements Mike, Chris, Larry, and I had helped to craft for *Good Old Boys*, aided toward integrating the group into John's stage show.

As the decade ended, new prospects led to the beginnings of a rejuvenation for John's career. Unfortunately, as the band improved, an old enemy cut into these opportunities. It's sad that this occurred just as the band began to jell.

Since the start of our friendship, John had been honest with me about his 1980 bout with cancer. However, what he hadn't revealed was the possibility and reality of the disease's recurrence. The more I was around John, the more I intuited that, from 1980 onward, he had dealt with regular returns of his malady. Sometime during the period of the formation for the Stringband, John acknowledged that his cancer was back. But for the moment, that information was to be kept private. However, by April 1999, John began mentioning onstage that he once again had the disease.

When John's diagnosis became more serious, it appeared to me that he had been prioritizing his life around his music. Restricting him to his home for six months or a year while the doctors blasted his illness was not realistic. John told them to treat him with just enough medications to beat back the cancer. The goal was to keep him functional, on stage, and on the road.

Luckily, as 1999 began, John was still in good voice and good spirits, resulting in some memorable gigs. March 6, John and the Stringband shared the bill at Wilkes Community College, the site of MerleFest, with Gillian Welch and David Rawlings.

Because of John's Missouri connections, there were multiple appearances in the spring and fall within the state. On April 3, we played in the morning over KDHX radio in St. Louis for *Down Yonder* with Keith Dudding. That evening, the Hartford Stringband was in St. Charles on the *Goldenrod* showboat at a benefit for the Daniel Boone Bicentennial events committee. Later that month, John returned to his hometown for the Community Fair at the Missouri History Museum. May 15–16 was a special weekend for John, as he was inducted into the St. Louis Walk of Fame. The Stringband played at the Duck Room, a venue created for musical legend Chuck Berry. Chuck and John even sat together at the luncheon celebrating the Walk of Fame honor. Our last Missouri gig of the year had John joining his old bandmates Norman Ford and Don Brown on September 17 in Wentzville for the Summer Music Festival.

There were lots of other travels that year. In early June, with Jamie Harford filling in for Mike Compton, we performed in Nashville at Gibson's Café Milano before heading north for two days at Churchill Downs. The landmark Louisville, Kentucky, racetrack had decided to hold a music festival in the infield, where we shared the stage with Retrograss member Mike Seeger. Leaving Nashville late at night after our Gibson's Café Milano gig, with John and the band asleep, Larry Perkins navigated the bus to the track. In the hour before daybreak, I awoke to Larry arguing with security about bringing our vehicle onto the infield. He succeeded in making his case and guided the bus through a tunnel under the racetrack. I exited the bus at dawn to the breathtaking sight of racehorses being exercised in the mist of early morning and later was able to tour the empty track at night.

As John had become more interested in the fiddle, he relished being in situations where he could play and discuss the instrument with like-minded people. Therefore, he was thrilled when Keith Case lined up a tour of the northwest United States and Canada that began at the Festival of American Fiddle Tunes. "Fiddle Tunes," as the event was better known, featured multiple fiddle styles taught and per-formed at Fort Worden Historical State Park in Port Townsend, Wash-ington, on the Olympic Peninsula. This weeklong gathering of music fanatics was held within the decommissioned barracks and buildings of a former army installation (where filming was done for 1982's *An Officer and a Gentleman*).

John took full advantage of the Fiddle Tunes experience. When outside of class, he jammed with students as well as instructors. John also absorbed the other musical styles featured, often witnessing late-night performances and jams. One direct result was his adoption of several fiddle tunes from the French-Canadian repertoire.

Since his introduction of the windows concept in 1995, John had been promoting that arrangement style to various musicians. This included John's band class in Port Townsend. Besides espousing windows to his students, John discussed the phrasing of a fiddle tune, creating tension and resolution by utilizing "three questions and an answer." This meant separating each of the first three four-bar sections for each part (the question asked three times) from the tune proper to emphasize the fourth phrase (the answer) and definitively end each section.

In addition to teaching our classes, John and the Hartford String-band performed twice: once for the students and faculty on Wednesday evening and at the close of the public concert on Friday, July 2. As one might expect, John chose to shelve his normal performing repertoire in favor of a selection of fiddle tunes from his three instrumental albums of the 1990s.

The two stage sets exploded with nervous energy, reflecting John's excitement at being in this fiddler's paradise. He can be heard on the recordings from those evenings talking throughout the sets, cueing the band toward what he wanted. The windows experiment yielded an almost Grateful Dead–style approach, stretching John's repertoire with solos and collective improvisations.

For the Friday show, we encored with "Squirrel Hunters." As the other band members fell away, I was given a showcase, encouraged by John, that transcended the limits of all my previous solos. At the time, it seemed to last ten or twenty minutes, although, in reality, it was only a fraction of that length.

With our performances at Port Townsend, John's use of windows as an arrangement device came to an end. John felt that he had taken the conceit as far as was useful, and it was time to move on. The band, apart from myself, agreed, and eagerly returned to normal soloing.

This trip was notable for several other reasons. One was that John had resumed smoking marijuana. He had quit the drug upon his first cancer diagnosis and hadn't imbibed for almost twenty years. However, John had recently decided to resume his marijuana use supposedly to counteract the side effects of his chemotherapy (this was before medical marijuana was legalized).

One of the consequences for John's dope smoking was his incessant desire to converse. The band shared a large duplex, with doorways connecting their kitchens and living rooms. John would tail whoever was trying to get away from his constant chatter in and out of each side of the residence. Since John and I were sharing one half with Chris and Mike in the other, Mike Compton would often lock the common doors to prevent John from following him around.

At the conclusion of Fiddle Tunes, while I produced a recording for guitarist/singer Del Rey, John, Chris, and Mike took a few days off in Seattle. For our next appearance, the Hartford Stringband split a concert at the Oregon Zoo in Portland with banjoist Alison Brown (whose record label would release the Stringband's John Hartford tribute after his passing). It was then back to Seattle for a night at the Tractor Tavern. The small club was standing room only (literally: most of the chairs had been removed to accommodate the large audience). My most vivid memory is of being blocked for the entire night from the microphone by John. I had committed the cardinal sin of (in John's mind) taking the spotlight away from him on the second song, resulting in his reducing my musical role for evening.

The next morning, we flew to Anchorage, Alaska. We spent twenty-four hours in the constant twilight for a concert opened and promoted by John's old friend, guitarist/singer Ginger Boatwright. Interestingly, upon a later move to Alaska by John's singing first wife, Betty, the two women allied for joint performances.

Finally, we headed to Canada for the second annual Musicfest, held on an extremely rural part of Vancouver Island. After an eternity of being detained at customs and a flight from the mainland on a rickety small plane, we made it to the one-horse town of Courtenay. There was so little to occupy one's offstage time that this was the only occasion I can remember fellow performer David Grier being glad to see us!

When we returned east at the end of the tour, John came down with a cold. It lasted through our two outdoor appearances in mid-July. One consequence was that John had a cough and his singing was a bit hoarse. The other was attempting to see how far he could push an audience. Rationalizing that this beat the alternative of a drippy nose, John performed with tissues hanging from his nostrils. Riverboat captain John Hartford became, in his words, "Captain Kleenex."

On a weekend swing through Michigan in September, we were sponsored at one location by a huge fan of John's music, whose family owned the local Buick dealership. After our daytime appearance, we were wined and dined at a French restaurant. With the band all seated around a table and our host ordering expensive bottles of spirits from the owner, I could tell that John, normally responsible for the band's meals, was beginning to get worried. Luckily, our benefactor had planned on picking up the check.

Our first appearances after the release of *Good Old Boys* were at Byron Berline's International Bluegrass Festival in Guthrie, Oklahoma. During this sojourn, John began reminiscing about how bluegrass groups like Flatt & Scruggs would send a few band members out into the audience to sell product while the rest of the ensemble would continue to play. We adopted that conceit during several sets, and I went out into the crowd to push the new recording.

Another bit of inspired stage business occurred at Tall Stacks, held on the Cincinnati waterfront. Since the first event in 1988, John had been a perennial favorite, appearing at every gathering until his passing. He even provided the steamboat festival with its theme song.

At the Tall Stacks in October 1995, before I had joined John's band but after we had begun our friendship, John, Mike Compton, and Roy Huskey Jr. on bass performed the national anthem during a Reds baseball game (at that time, Cincinnati was contesting Atlanta for a place in the World Series). Much to my chagrin, even though I was at the festival and the only baseball fan among us, I was not invited to go along!

During the 1999 steamboat gathering held in mid-October, the Hartford Stringband played across the river over WNKU-FM in

Covington, Kentucky. There, John revived (and stumped the band with) his unique banjo arrangement of "Little Cabin Home on the Hill," previously recorded for *True Life Blues*.

One evening at the conclusion of our performance, John, myself, and my (at the time) three-year-old son, Benjamin, who was with me for that week, took a ride on the stern wheel towboat the *Allegheny*. John got into a discussion with Captain Nelson Jones, and they decided to have us include the boat during our riverside set on Saturday. While playing the John Hartford song "M.I.S.S.I.P." I contacted the captain on my cellphone. Through the phone connection, John entertained the audience by conducting several signaling whistles by the boat.

A third piece of planned mayhem occurred at the Station Inn in Nashville. John had adopted Marie's grandson Dustin, who, at the time, was training to become a professional wrestler. In the middle of one of his sets at the Station, John had Dustin and another student wrestler start a fight in the audience. The crowd was (of course) unaware that the brawl wasn't real and were stunned into silence. John had to stop and explain about the history of conflicts in the "rough" country bars of his youth and how he had come up with this approximation to recreate that experience for the Station Inn's audience. And then, he had the two scrap again.

As should be obvious from the earlier parts of John's career, he loved this sort of "stage business." Some, like the controlling of whistles, were planned. Others, such as the story that follows, occurred more spontaneously.

For a reason I can't recall, just John, driver Jimmy Johnson, and I made the trip to the 20th Anniversary Thomas Point Beach Bluegrass Festival in Maine in August 1997. Harking back to our Japanese tour, I accompanied John during his two sets on banjo and guitar.

The elevated mainstage was backed with a wall containing two doorways, each with steps leading from the ground to stage level. I guess the intentions of whoever designed the platform assumed that, as an act would be leaving by one entrance, the next performers could ascend to the stage through the other without causing a traffic jam.

The Lewis Family gospel bluegrass group was scheduled to follow us and were watching John's set from the openings in the backdrop.

After John spied them, he launched extemporaneously into a rap about how, when he died, he wanted the Lewis sisters (there were three: "Miggie," Polly, and Janis) to sing John's song ("Hey, Babe, you want to") "Boogie" at his funeral. John then looked right at them and I, swept up in the moment, motioned them to come to the microphones. To which they emphatically shook their heads. Somehow, we managed to get the three sisters to sing "Boogie" on mic, the words of which, interestingly, they knew. As soon as they began, John lay down and crossed his arms like he was laid out in his coffin. I think some flowers appeared as well and were placed across his chest. It was one of the funniest things I'd ever seen. Even though I was onstage, I couldn't stop laughing throughout the rest of the song.

John's year of performances concluded with a relaxed appearance at the Red Light Café in Atlanta, Georgia. The Hartford Band played multiple times at the Red Light; John was an audience favorite at the club, and he consistently sold out this intimate, informal venue.

Oh, I get it, you're a tourist.

Early in 1999, Rounder Records asked me to locate the session tapes for John's *Gum Tree Canoe* recordings. The label had purchased Flying Fish Records, which originally issued the album, and wanted to release an expanded version on CD. I supervised the mixes for the outtakes, "You Asked Me To" and "I Wonder Where You Are Tonight," which were then added to their release.

Two years earlier, Rounder had licensed John's *Aereo-Plain* record from Warner Bros. They contacted John about those original session tapes, which, at the time, were missing. Neither he nor Rounder knew that the masters resided in the garage of Tompall Glaser, John's publisher and studio owner for the *Aereo-Plain* recording sessions. By 1999, Glaser was moving and had sent all the *Aereo* tapes over to John.

So, when John took me to the third floor of his home to pull the *Gum Tree* recordings, there were also eighty-plus reels from *Aereo-Plain* in his tape library. When I saw the *Aereo* LP material, I asked, "John, what's this?" He replied, "Oh, shit, Ken Irwin [one of Rounder's owners at that time] is going to be pissed with me." Therefore, in addition to supervising the *Gum Tree Canoe* CD, I also ended up assembling a collection of outtakes for Rounder Records from *Aereo-Plain*. Either John had no interest in revisiting these recordings, was too busy with new material and projects he was rushing to complete while he was still functioning or trusted me to make all the decisions. The only request that John made was to exclude "Smoke, Shit and F**k" from the issued outtakes.

By January 2000, I had mastered what came to be called *Steam Powered Aereo-Takes*. The final CD included material rejected by producer David Bromberg, Hartford song demos, and an unreleased Aereo-Plain Band single from early 1972.

For 1999, some changes were made by John to his performing repertoire. Chief among them was to reintroduce his "Delta Queen Waltz." Additionally, John had been featuring the fiddle tune "Squirrel Hunters" since the band's formation and continued to perform pieces from Ed Haley's extensive repertoire. Two other instrumentals were "Benny Martin Special #2" and "Reel D'Issoudun" (which John jokingly referred to onstage as "Reel of Esso Gasoline"). The latter was one of the French-Canadian pieces John had learned at the Festival of American Fiddle Tunes; the former John had based on an improvisation by Benny. The "#2" was a joke by John to infer that there were more than one Special (there weren't).

With his focus shifting to the fiddle, all John's banjo songs were phased out of our sets except for "Gum Tree Canoe," "Lorena," and "Short Life of Trouble." Additionally, John revived "Old Time River Man" as well as "Little Cabin Home on the Hill" from *True Life Blues*. John also eliminated all his guitar-backed songs, ending his use of the instrument onstage during our July tour.

There were two things that eventually promoted visibility and audience recognition for Mike, Chris, Larry, and me. One was the development of distinct onstage personalities by each of the Hartford Stringband members. The manifestations for these differences are best defined by the way we dressed.

Obviously, when he formed the Hartford Stringband, John already had a personalized image. John called the Victorian riverboat captain "costume" of derby, vest, white shirt, and spectator or capped toe shoes his "character" or "clown suit." This nomenclature was in reference,

I believe, to the distinct personalities and, therefore, costumes and makeup, utilized by circus performers. Up until the time when I first began performing with John, all his backup musicians echoed these derby/vest identifiers. Jerry McCoury, in his short tenure with John, incurred his displeasure by donning a vest evoking the flocked wallpaper from an 1890s house of ill repute.

I already had a well-defined stage character and outfit from fifteen years of solo performing. Therefore, I couldn't understand the wisdom of matching the outfits of the other members of the Stringband. At an early gig with McCoury and Mike Compton sartorially mimicking John's attire, I refused to wear a derby and insisted instead on a straw skimmer. My later summer stage clothes of Hawaiian shirt, straw hat, and sunglasses prompted John to remark, "Oh, I get it, you're a tourist" (as John described me in his song, "She's Gone [And Bob's Gone with Her]": "Bob's got the hat and the loud Hawaiian shirt / Bob's got the two-tone shoes").

My vintage look was joined by Chris Sharp's adopting a hat, shirt, and shoes à la the 1950s Flatt & Scruggs band, with Mike Compton and Larry Perkins choosing bib overalls. Mike accessorized his bibs with a vintage tie, while Larry elected to add a suit jacket for that "farmer going to church on Sunday" look.

The second factor that promoted visibility for the Stringband was John's onstage recognition of our presence. He spotlighted the individual band members through nightly features. These solo spots were included to emphasize the group's talents, create a traveling variety show atmosphere, as well as to spell John on those nights when his cancer and its treatment were negatively affecting him.

Depending on the evening, Mike would perform a Bill Monroe or original mandolin tune or sing a blues backed by tenor guitar. Chris would feature a composition off his album or something out of the Flatt & Scruggs songbook. Larry Perkins would pick the banjo behind John's "The Boys from North Carolina" or on an Earl Scruggs piece. Sometimes, Larry picked up a guitar to render a Carter Family or Joseph Spence tune. Since I had left solo performing to join John's ensemble, I often featured something from my "act." Examples were a traditional banjo song or something from the Beatles within my spot. For the most part, John was generous in sharing us with his audiences. He often told us, "You're welcome to use my brand—'John Hartford'—to your advantage."

There was a dearth of newly released John Hartford projects in 2000. The lone exception was a live, archival greatest hits package from the *Mountain Stage* radio program (released by Blue Plate Music).

> There's a feller in there that'll pay you ten dollars if you sing into his can
>
> —TIM BLAKE NELSON, AS DELMAR O'DONNELL IN *O BROTHER, WHERE ART THOU?*

The biggest news for John in the year 2000 was the release of the movie and soundtrack album *O Brother, Where Art Thou?* In early 1999, John had been contacted by Joel and Ethan Coen about participating in their filmed version of the classic Greek poet Homer's epic narrative the *Odyssey*. The Coen brothers had recast the story in the Depression-era American South and enlisted him to perform on the soundtrack, even offering John a small acting role in the film.

John and I were both huge fans of the Coens' work, and, therefore, when he phoned me to share the news, I was visibly excited (we had no idea that the movie would achieve popular success). However, the Coens, unaware of John's recent work with the Stringband, had only extended the offer to him. Mike, Chris, Larry, and I were not invited to participate in the filming or in the recording of the score. And John, claiming that he didn't want to jinx the deal, wouldn't mention the existence of his regular group to Joel and Ethan. The most John would extend himself was to invite Mike, Chris, and myself (but not Larry Perkins) to accompany him to the first *O Brother* recording session to be held in Nashville at the end of April.

Unfortunately for me, the meeting coincided with MerleFest, where I'd been hired to perform outside of my role with John and the Hartford Stringband. Mike and Chris went along with John to the gathering, which resulted in their inclusion.

That summer, Larry Perkins drove the bus with Marie and John as passengers down to view the location filming done outside of Marie's hometown of Jackson, Mississippi. However, when it was time to shoot John's scene in Los Angeles, he was too ill to fly to California. Instead, David Holt was hired to (literally) fill the (dancing) shoes of John Hartford.

The Coens celebrated the music of *O Brother* with a concert in May 2000 at the Ryman Auditorium in Nashville. John emceed and was backed by Mike, Chris, and Larry. Since I wasn't on the soundtrack, I wasn't included. Larry, who lived in Nashville, decided to participate without any guarantees of inclusion or payment. In October, the film premiered and by December, both the concert video and accompanying album, titled *Down from the Mountain*, hit the stores. The *O Brother, Where Art Thou?* soundtrack went on to win a Grammy award for Album of the Year, at the same time the live *Down from the Mountain* CD captured Best Traditional Folk Album. This exposure for John reinvigorated his career. If he had survived his cancer and returned to full strength, in a few years John would have been center stage as the face for all musical events *O Brother*.

I KNOW WHY EVERYBODY'S HERE; THEY THINK I'M GONNA CROAK

Before *O Brother, Where Art Thou?* became a phenomenon, John's touring continued as before. His advancing cancer affected his voice and energy level, and his ability to execute a performance suffered as well. Instead of standing, more shows were completed with at least John and, sometimes, the whole band, sitting down. For an April 1 appearance at the Fireman's Kitchen in Hickory, North Carolina, John slept onstage between sets. Concerned about his weakening immune system, John decided to stop signing autographs.

However, something within John needed to be onstage, acting out his fight with the disease in front of his fans. John took something from his supporters. They kept him going and fed John's musical experiments. And his loyal admirers, possibly realizing that John's time was limited, received something back from seeing him however compromised his condition.

John and the Hartford Stringband made three trips to the St. Louis area in 2000. The first was during the last weekend of February. John received the Capt. Donald T. Wright Award in Maritime Journalism at the Mercantile Library, where we also performed. Although lacking much voice, John turned in spirited concerts for his return to KDHX

L to r: Bob Carlin, Mike Compton, John Hartford, Larry Perkins, Chris Sharp. April 1, 2000, Acoustic Stage, Fireman's Kitchen, Hickory, NC. The progression of John's cancer necessitated Hartford and his band sitting for this performance. Collection of the author.

and the Duck Room, sharing onstage tunes with local stringband the Ill-Mo Boys. By that time, Mike Compton had been asked to rejoin the Nashville Bluegrass Band. Therefore, the John Hartford show in June at the Missouri Botanical Gardens would feature Mike's substitute, Matt Combs. Mike thereafter split his attention between the NBB and the Hartford Stringband. Our last Missouri show for the year was a fall weekend at the Wildwood Springs Lodge. Fiddler Cecil Goforth (brother to Gene), one of John's old musical mentors, came and sat in with the band.

At the end of April, John was brought back to MerleFest for his seventh and final appearance. In advance of Sunday's mainstage tribute, John and the band participated in the fiddle and banjo duets as well as fiddle workshops. John et al. also played three small stage sets that weekend, with our strongest performance held in a rainstorm. With John running a group of songs and tunes into a long medley, the Hartford Stringband shifted into overdrive. He led the audience through "Good Old Boys" to introduce the band, and on to "Arkansas Traveler," "Opera Reel," and "Gentle on My Mind" before topping the set off with "Sally Goodin."

John Hartford and the Hartford Stringband, l to r: Bob Carlin, Mike Compton, Larry Perkins, John Hartford, Chris Sharp. April 28–30, 2000, MerleFest, Wilkesboro, NC. John and the Hartford Stringband appear as a part of a tribute to John held on the festival's mainstage. Photograph by Frank Serio/Frank Serio Photography.

For Sunday's appearance, as John would do for another homage later that year, he chose to spotlight his influences. Included that afternoon were "Me and My Fiddle" from Benny Martin; "The Cross-Eyed Child," John's song about Bill Monroe; and "The Boys From North Carolina," exalting Earl Scruggs.

Summer touring took John and the Hartford Stringband to the Grey Fox Bluegrass Festival, the Lake Champlain Maritime Museum in Vermont, as well as out west to Bozeman, Montana, on a double bill with the Del McCoury Band. At the RockyGrass festival outside of Boulder, Colorado, John also appeared with Retrograss. By this point in time, John had narrowed his repertoire to the minimal list of material that he needed to get through each concert.

While we were on a trip to the RockyGrass, John was approached by the wife of a fellow musician. She beseeched him to try alternative therapies to cure his cancer (this being Boulder, after all). John became agitated and fussed about her advice for most of that day, as, by then, John was done with unconventional medical practices, adhering to traditional treatments for his cancer. After all, his father had been a

John Hartford and the Hartford Stringband, l to r: Bob Carlin, Mike Compton, Larry Perkins (hidden), John Hartford, Chris Sharp. July 14–15, 2000, Grey Fox Bluegrass Festival, Oak Hill, NY. Two views/ two sides of the Stringband: at an informal, afternoon set (in "street clothes") and performing for an evening concert (wearing "stage clothes"). Photograph by Frank Serio/Frank Serio Photography.

doctor, a man of science, and John was following what his dad would have recommended.

While we were in Boulder, John was paid a visit by fiddler Jim "Texas Shorty" Chancellor. After jamming back at the hotel, he included Shorty in our mainstage set and workshop appearance. Under the small tent, rather than focus on his own playing John turned the spotlight on Chancellor. Shorty was always a technically proficient player. However, on this particular afternoon, with the Stringband backing him up, Shorty just lit up and played the fire out of a group of fiddle tunes. It felt as if Shorty was inspired by John's friendship and wanted to honor him by doing his absolute best.

PREDNISONE PROJECTS

Over a year had passed since the *Good Old Boys* sessions, and John appeared ready to make another album. At the end of April, he introduced his ideas to the Stringband via the usual route of a work tape demo. During a weekend of Atlanta gigs June 2 and 3, John held the first rehearsals for his projected new recording.

John titled the project *Old Family Jig* after one of his original songs earmarked for inclusion. Other original (some working) titles included "I Do Like Licker," "They Can't Outshine Me and You," "This Ain't No Way Livin' This A-Way," "In Case I Run into You," "One Man's Trash Is Another Man's Treasure," and "Papaw's Down with the Blues." All these songs used original fiddle instrumentals to provide the melody for soloing instead of the sung melody from each song. For example, "Papaw" utilized John's "Homer the Roamer" for the breaks. Except for the traditional fiddle tune "East Tennessee Blues," to which John had written words, the windows method of albums past had gone by the wayside.

For a long time, John had been a lover of Irish, Scottish, and British fiddle music. However, this was the first time John had written a whole collection of songs and tunes with such a strong Celtic flavor.

But when presented with an album outside of their musical experience, Chris, Mike, and Larry were puzzled. Although the band sounded better than they felt they did on these selections, as rehearsals proceeded, their frustration level rose.

In response, John presented the Stringband with some additional material more (as John would say) in their wheelhouse. These included the bluegrass, blues, and Hartfordesque "Dear Old Dixie" (with words by John), the gospel song "Beautiful Raindrops on a Pie Plate of Glass," "Snake Face Blues," "Madison, Tennessee," and "She's Gone (And Bob's Gone with Her)."

I was with John on the tour bus when he was working on those last compositions. John once explained to me that his songs were by no means about one specific person or incident and that he never tried to transcribe his life line by line. Rather, he would take bits and pieces from various events and combine them into a pastiche.

Each verse of "Madison," John explained, had a different genesis. Verse one ("the rag I borrowed somewhere, to wipe my bloodshot nose") dated back to John's sinus surgery and its aftereffects. Verse two ("I put my finger on a map") referred to a time when John asked us how long it would take to get back to Nashville after a gig. Verse three ("Out behind the firehouse") was about the famous jam sessions in a house rented by Larry Perkins from Earl Scruggs. Located on the other side of Gallatin Road from the Hartford home, Larry's unassuming dwelling drew the *crème de la crème* of bluegrass musicians. I also noticed the influence of the Osborne Brothers hit "Rocky Top" on bits of the melody and structure of "Madison, Tennessee."

On the other hand, "She's Gone (And Bob's Gone with Her)" was based on an event of which I was at the unfortunate center. Ironically, John told me he was working on a new song and asked did I want to hear it. He then sang the "Bob's got the hat" verse. After a pregnant pause, John said, "But it's not about you," when it obviously was inspired by real life. Fortunately, as I was married at the time with a young son, the woman in the song ran off with someone else other than me. I had always wished that John would put me into one of his songs. However, this was a case of "Be careful of what you wish for, it might come true!"

At this point in his illness, John had become extremely emotionally vulnerable and looked to his band to support this new collection of material. I attempted to encourage him to move forward with the recording. John was a fan of *The Gathering*, an album of Celtic infused compositions written, produced, and performed by Grey Larsen. I felt that John would benefit from the experience of working with Grey and suggested that he assemble a group of Celtic musicians to reinforce the Stringband.

Album rehearsals continued throughout June and July, although, from this vantage point, it is unclear what exactly was attempted. Ultimately, it became apparent to John that Chris, Mike, and Larry's validation wasn't forthcoming. John came to believe that the *Old Family Jig* material was too complex and, therefore, would prove inaccessible for the listening public. By July's end, influenced by his reservations along with his deteriorating health, John shelved *Old Family Jig*.

This is an album of memories

Instead, John decided to pay tribute to the fiddle heroes of his youth from back home in Missouri.

During the late 1950s and early 1960s, John had hauled around a Wollensak tape machine to collect fiddle tunes from some of his favorite musicians. At that time, he planned to use these documents to expand his repertoire. By the 1990s, without a functioning reel-to-reel machine, John could no longer revisit these recordings. Therefore, he passed them along to prominent country music researcher, author, and Hartford friend (the late) Dr. Charles Wolfe. A chance meeting at the end of 1999 between Wolfe and Jim Nelson prompted Dr. Wolfe to give the tapes to him. Jim was known to John through Nelson's membership in the Ill-Mo Boys. Jim was also scholar with an interest in Missouri traditions.

After copying John's fiddle tapes onto CD, Jim shared the dubs in early 2000. This inspired John to assemble a tune list for what became his final project. After the abortive attempt at *Old Family Jig*, honoring the Missouri fiddlers and fiddle repertoire became the obvious choice for John's next recording.

As with *Good Old Boys*, the sessions for what became *Hamilton Ironworks* were shoehorned in between gigs. The album was recorded quickly in mid-August 2000 at Overdub Lane studios in Durham, North Carolina. Over a day and a half, engineer Wes Lachot committed our performances to digital. Except for a few banjo over-dubs by Larry Perkins, everything was cut live in the studio.

John referred to this and other undertakings during this period as "prednisone projects." His cancer and its treatment had often left him lethargic or with low-grade viruses. To counteract his condition, John's doctors gave him bouts of steroids. These provided John with bursts of energy. Therefore, he tried to schedule his creative work to coincide with these energetic boosts.

Judging from the session reels, it was a relaxed, amiable affair. John sounds relatively at ease and happy. The band sounds good, but mistakes increase over the compressed recording schedule.

Rather than the windows method or the soloing that followed it on stage, John requested for *Hamilton Ironworks* that the band stay behind him. John was to take the lead throughout the recordings. He alternated stories about each tune with the fiddle melodies over the chord changes we provided.

Three years earlier, John had honored Gene Goforth by accompanying and recording Gene for an album of traditional tunes. Released by Rounder Records, *Emminence Breakdown* [sic] was John's tribute to Gene's formative musical influence. John continued to honor him by duplicating thirteen of Gene's tunes for his own collection of Missouri fiddle music. The additional twelve recorded pieces (three were ultimately discarded) came from other sources such as Roy Wooliver and Homer Dillard.

John had previously released two of the tunes committed to tape for *Hamilton Ironworks*. "Hi Dad in the Morning," which he had learned from Douglas and Rodney Dillard's father, appeared on *Dillard Hartford Dillard Glitter Grass* in 1977. John and I recorded "Greenback Dollar" for 1994's *The Fun of Open Discussion*. He had played "Hamilton Ironworks," supposedly composed by Wooliver, as long as John and I had known each other. Most of the other tunes had been attempted at some point in the last five to ten years.

As the year ended and John's touring slowed, we were able to complete the mixes and notes for *Hamilton*. On December 1, 2000, John was handed a CD of proposed finished tracks and I was ready to take the album for mastering.

Perhaps it was the steroids or the rally that often occurs in terminally ill patients approaching life's end. Whatever was the cause, after deteriorating for the first part of the year, John made a strong midsummer comeback. He gained weight and his voice returned.

On Saturday, August 26, the Hartford Stringband, with Chris Thiele subbing for Mike Compton, took the mainstage at the Philadelphia Folk Festival. (The bus had broken down on the way to the event, and we had to leave Mike behind to supervise repairs.) John, ironically replacing Bruce "Utah" Phillips, who was too ill to perform, played a strong set of favorites. Ed Haley fiddle tunes, "Steam Powered Aereo Plane," "Gentle on My Mind," and "Watching the River Go By" were offered in vibrant versions. John was standing, present, focused, and funny. He ended on the banjo, played a transformative "Foggy Mountain Landscape," and then went back to the festival hotel to jam into the early morning hours.

It appeared that John might actually be winning his cancer battle.

However, this quickly became a temporary reprieve. For September's trips to Utah and Idaho with Ramblin' Jack Elliott, as well as at a festival in Illinois with Del McCoury, John lacked energy and voice and was back to sitting down. He dragged through appearances at the International Bluegrass Festival and the Tennessee Fall Homecoming, as well as braving a snowstorm for a trip to South Dakota and Missouri. John was a shadow of his former self leading a November reunion of the Aereo-Plain Band. Held at the Troy (New York) Music Hall, backup for Norman Blake, Tut Taylor, Vassar Clements, and John were provided by the Stringband and Sam Bush.

The requests for Norman, Tut, Vassar, and John to reenact the acclaimed *Aereo-Plain* album began as early as 1974. In April of that year, the four musicians joined producer David Bromberg and *Morning Bugle* bassist Dave Holland (who John later told me, in hindsight, should have been on his first Warner Bros. album as well) at Philadelphia's Academy of Music. Besides Troy, John, Tut, and Vassar, with Tony Rice subbing for the absent Norman, performed in 1994 at the Ryman Auditorium in Nashville. A recording of that event was included in the book *Pilot of a Steam Powered Aereo-Plain*, a posthumous volume authored by Andrew Vaughan for the Hartford estate.

John Hartford and the Hartford Stringband, l to r: Bob Carlin, John Hartford, Mike Compton, Chris Sharp, Larry Perkins. September 24, 2000, A Tribute to John Hartford, Live from Mountain Stage, War Memorial Auditorium, Nashville, TN. John headlined this all-star tribute recorded for radio broadcast and later released on compact disc. Photograph by David Schenk.

One of John's last hurrahs was the John Hartford tribute concert at the War Memorial Auditorium in Nashville. Sponsored and recorded by the *Mountain Stage* radio program, the location held special significance for John (the War Memorial had been one of the past locations for the Grand Ole Opry). Country star Kathy Mattea, Tim O'Brien, western group Riders in the Sky, Gillian Welch and David Rawlings from the *O Brother* and *Down from the Mountain* soundtracks, Norman Blake of the Aereo-Plain Band, John's son Jamie Harford, as well as Bela Fleck and other ex–New Grass Revival members John Cowan and Pat Flynn all honored John's contribution to music.

When his turn came, John, as he had at the MerleFest tribute earlier that year, diverted the attention to Monroe, Martin, and Scruggs. After expressing his heartfelt gratitude to everyone for honoring him "if for no other reason, coming out and validating what I've been doing for all these years," with his typical humor, John told the assembled (to great laughter and tremendous applause):

I know why everybody's here; they think I'm gonna croak. Now, everybody here tonight has done their part. And, if I was to do my part, I should wait for about three weeks while it's still fresh on everybody's mind and then kick off! But we got the whole month of October booked, so, I can't do that.

On December 16, John and the Hartford Stringband made our last appearance of 2000 at Atlanta's Red Light Cafe. At some point between mid-November and this performance, John had ceased playing the banjo. At the Red Light, John performed sitting down. His voice was very hoarse; John offered no spoken intros to the selections. All in all, this was a very low-energy night. What no one knew at this point was that this would be one of the last times that John would be able to play a musical instrument. What was unthinkable for John and the Stringband was that no matter how bad things seemed, they would get much worse in the new year.

"Give Me the Flowers While I'm Living"

John's first documented performance of 2001 was on January 26. Without my presence, John and the Stringband appeared on the Friday Grand Ole Opry. My first appearance would be about a month later. On March 1, I met the group for a concert sponsored by the International Propeller Club, a maritime organization, on the steamboat *Belle of Cincinnati*. It was my debut Stringband gig with Matt Combs substituting for Mike Compton, as well as the first time I was to witness John's loss of ability to play an instrument.

As 2001 unfolded, John's cancer continued attacking his nervous system. Lesions on his nerve sheath prevented commands from John's brain reaching his left arm; by the spring, John would also lose control of his right arm. Appearances became farewell performances, with the Stringband providing most of the music. John would sit on stage calling the tunes, doing his best to talk and sing. The big question became, How long would John be able to continue? The stress of carrying around a terminally ill musician was affecting the band members as well.

Without the use of his hands, John required full-time care. He needed help with dressing, eating, and with all other daily functions. Within a normally functioning household, medical insurance would have covered the nursing aids necessary to look after someone in John's condition. Or his care would have been administered within a specialized facility. However, neither John nor Marie trusted his support to anyone outside his immediate circle of family and employees. So Marie and her children looked after John's needs at home; and it was expected that the band members would do the same while John was on the road.

Mike Compton, now fully integrated back into the Nashville Bluegrass Band, was sometimes absent. It was fortunate, in a perverse way, that Matt Combs, brought in to substitute for Mike on the mandolin, was primarily a fiddler, and could cover John's parts on that instrument. Although still dedicated to performing with John, I was being pulled away by commitments to four outside album projects, as well as shepherding *Hamilton Ironworks* and the CD reissue of *Gum Tree Canoe* to completion. In addition to continuing to perform with the Hartford Stringband as well as Black fiddler Joe Thompson, I also had familial obligations to fulfill, including providing supervision for my young son.

Therefore, I wasn't available to ride the bus to and from appearances and care for John. The brunt of that responsibility fell hard on my bandmates Chris Sharp, Matt Combs, and Larry Perkins.

THANKS FOR COMING TO SEE US, WHEN YOU COULD HAVE BEEN ELSEWHERE INSTEAD.

John had six nights of appearances booked in March, including in Ohio; Pittsburgh, Pennsylvania; and Asheville, North Carolina. I drove my own vehicle to play on five of them. John could now only hold an instrument onstage (which he was unable to play) and became weaker as the month progressed. Surprisingly, he was still entertaining and, with support from the Stringband and other guest musicians, able to hold an audience's attention.

However, by the time John brought his show to Asheville at the end of the month, his diminished skills resulted in the onset of negative

John Hartford and the Hartford Stringband. Sitting: John Hartford; l to r, standing: Bob Carlin, Matt Combs, Chris Sharp, Larry Perkins. April 7, 2001, Old Settler's Music Festival, Dale, TX. John was extremely weak and unfocused, which somewhat shows in this photograph. With guests Nickel Creek joining us onstage, this was to be John's last performance. Photograph by Jim Dirden.

reviews published by local newspapers. Audiences as well had become painfully aware that they were witnessing the last hurrah of John Hartford. Some fans were honored and grateful to be in attendance. Unfortunately, growing numbers, expecting a John Hartford show of years previous, felt that they had been duped into paying good money to see the shadow of his former self. Unaware that John wanted to spend his final days onstage with those who had supported him for over thirty years, other attendees processed his condition with anger and disappointment.

April's opening weekend brought the John Hartford show to the Old Settler's Music Festival outside of Austin, Texas. While the rest of the band rode the nine hundred miles from Nashville on John's bus, I flew with my family to nearby Austin and drove by automobile out to the event site.

April 7 was spent getting John ready for his evening performance. He was extremely weak and unfocused, which somewhat shows in the backstage photo session for *Bluegrass Unlimited* completed that afternoon by Jim Dirden.

For John's Saturday evening set, the Stringband, with guests Chris Thiele and the Watkins siblings' band Nickel Creek and Todd Phillips on bass, gamely sat on stage and, prompted by John, entertained him and the audience as best we could. Luckily, some of the crowd were aware that they were witnessing what turned out to be the last public appearance by a dying man and gave John a positive response. Within the sadness, there was still some joy from a performer who had lived for the audience and the stage.

Unfortunately, a portion of those expected to be entertained and were sorely disappointed by John's lack of ability to deliver a John Hartford show. At the end of the performance, I drove back to Austin and flew home to North Carolina several days later.

I was informed afterward that the return trip to Nashville was somewhat chaotic, as the extremely ill Hartford insisted on checking himself into a hospital in Arkansas. Just as quickly, he checked himself out. Upon his arrival at home, John did end up in the Sarah Cannon Cancer Center in Nashville for two weeks to receive treatment for pneumonia.

Then, it was back home to spend the majority of John's remaining days in residence on the Cumberland River. The five scheduled May gigs were cancelled, along with appearances in June, August, and September.

Instead, as has been described in other accounts, from the end of April through May, a flood of musicians made their way to John's abode to serenade him. Musician Jim Rooney described this outpouring to Art Menius as akin to John and Marie Hartford's Christmas parties, "with lots of food [and] music, [but] no plan."

For those last weeks, I stayed in Nashville, providing help and support to John and the Hartford family. He had wanted to stay in familiar surroundings. When the end came, John planned to die in the front room of the house facing his beloved Cumberland River.

However, the reality of his demise put John back into the hospital. He spent several days under heavy sedation fighting the urge to let go. Around midday on June 4, 2001, when I sensed that the end was near, I left Marie and her eldest daughter with John and drove the short distance from the hospital to Gruhn Guitars. As I entered George's second-floor office, the phone rang to tell him that John had passed away.

I'm Batman.

Marie Hartford decided to follow Southern tradition and have John's coffin displayed in the front room of their home. For two days, John lay in state in an open casket for visitation by his friends and associates.

There is one famous rumor from John's funeral that has become an urban myth, that of "the batman cape." I will share what I witnessed and came to understand from Marie and her family, who helped take care of John and the Hartford homestead in the final weeks that John was alive.

Marie had opted to meet with the funeral directors in advance of John's passing to plan his memorial service. She chose the suit for him to wear but didn't want to upset John by informing him of her plans. So, Marie hid the garments in a closet. Of course, John happened to come into the room when the suit was being taken out for the undertakers. To avoid distressing John, the clothing was hurriedly returned to the cupboard and hidden within a Halloween costume that happened to be stored within. When, finally, the outfit was passed to the funeral home, the costume's Batman cape was included. One can just imagine the confusion and discussion that followed (after all, this is John Hartford).

Ultimately, John was dressed in the suit of clothes, with the Batman cape firmly fastened around his neck. This was all revealed when his body was returned to the house before the viewing. Of course, in another attempt by John to control the situation from the great beyond, his coffin wouldn't fit inside without the removal of the front door. Ultimately, the casket had to be stood upright to pass through the portal. Once set up in the living room, Marie and her daughter were brought in to view John. Chris Sharp and I were in the next room waiting our turns, and we were greeted with laughter. When I inquired what was so funny, I was told the story and shown the cape.

A Celebration of Life

John Cowan Hartford

December 30, 1937 – June 4, 2001

Program cover, *A Celebration of Life*, Madison, TN, June 8, 2001. Held on the grounds of John's home, a cornucopia of Nashville's finest pickers and singers rendered the greatest hits from John's output plus many of his traditional favorites. Photograph by Happy Traum. Collection of the author.

Naturally, the funeral directors were horrified that they'd made such a gaffe and wanted to immediately move John back to their facility to remove the cape. However, the mistake was easily rectified by shoving the offending garment underneath John, where it was hidden from sight. To the best of my knowledge, he was buried wearing the costume.

At the time, and to this day, I believe that the cape was John's revenge from the other side. He was so annoyed at being buried in a suit instead of his usual stage clothes that he willed the cape to appear.

For the viewing on June 6 and 7, 2001, the Hartford residence was filled with friends, family, and musicians paying their respects to the departed performer. On Friday, June 8, a memorial service was held on the grounds of John's home. At Marie's request and direction, Chris Sharp planned and arranged the memorial, which commenced at 2:00 p.m. John had kept a stash of moonshine, which, following his instructions, I dispensed to the assembled musicians.

After the steamboat *General Jackson* passed the house on the Cumberland, giving a hail on its whistle, words of welcome came from Cindy Sinclair, who had first met John when they crewed together on the *Julia Belle Swain*. After Sinclair came an outpouring of music hosted by WSM's Eddie Stubbs. A cornucopia of Nashville's finest pickers and singers rendered the greatest hits from John's output plus many of his traditional favorites. Luminaries performing from all aspects of John's life included members of the two Hartford Stringbands, the Osborne Brothers, the Nashville Bluegrass Band, Sam Bush and David Grisman, Gillian Welch and David Rawlings with Emmylou Harris, Earl Scruggs, and Jerry Douglas, as well as Tim O'Brien and Darrell Scott. Speeches about John's personal impact were followed by the assembled singing of "I'll Fly Away" to close out the proceedings. John was then interned in the Spring Hill Cemetery by the Cumberland River.

Sadly, Marie Hartford wasn't far behind John. Just six months later, she also succumbed to cancer, dying on his birthday. Marie was buried beside her spouse; a gazebo graces their area where one can sit and visit. The Hartfords' tombstone was designed by Western artist William Matthews, whose long association with John included painting the cover illustration for *Mark Twang*. (Matthews's most recent work is his mural crowning Fort Worth's Dickies Arena.)

On June 13, a week after his funeral, the musicians from *O Brother, Where Art Thou?* assembled at New York's Carnegie Hall. John had been tapped to emcee the reunion, and, if he had lived, his career would have been relaunched by *O Brother*. Instead, the concert became an epitaph for the deceased musician.

A month after John's death, *Hamilton Ironworks* and *A Tribute to John Hartford* were released. And even though I'd submitted a master of *Aereo-Takes* in 2000, Rounder Records waited until 2002 to issue it. There were several other efforts to honor John following his departure. These included a namesake festival founded by John's childhood friend John Hotze, who has also since passed on. The John Hartford Memorial Festival has continued in Hotze's absence, and other efforts have endured to promote John's music. Various musicians have produced tribute recordings, beginning with his son Jamie Harford's *A Part of Your History* in 2014. Since that time, recorded homages include Robert Ellis and Courtney Hartman's *Dear John* (Refuge Foundation for the Arts, 2017), *On the Road: A Tribute to John Hartford* (LoHi Records, 2020), and, most recently, Sam Bush's CD *Radio John: Songs of John Hartford* (Smithsonian Folkways, 2022).

However, in the years since John's death, there seemed to be limited interest in his former band from promoters and the public. Since 2001, Mike and Chris worked on a variety of *O Brother/Down from the Mountain* projects produced by T Bone Burnett. Larry Perkins found employment with an assortment of groups and Matt Combs joined the band of Opry regular Mike Snider. When my association with John Hartford ended, folks in the music biz stopped taking my calls and offers of record production dried up. It took me five years to build back my solo career to the level it had been before the Hartford Stringband.

Except for several all-star tributes, no one wanted to hear the Hartford Stringband playing John's music. Instead, everyone wanted John's performances of his songs. And, sadly, he wasn't available to take advantage of those requests.

It took the tenth anniversary of his passing for the John Hartford Stringband to reunite for several years of performances. After considering the idea of reviving the *Old Family Jig* compositions shelved during John's lifetime, several of John's songs and tunes written for that CD were instead rendered for the album *Memories of John*. Produced by bandmember Chris Sharp, the collection also included some of the band's Hartford favorites.

Matt Combs arranged the use of a classroom at Vanderbilt's Blair School of Music, where he taught in Nashville. Chris brought along his mobile studio and engineer David Arnold. Special guests Alison Brown, George Buckner, Bela Fleck, Tim O'Brien, Alan O'Bryant, and Eileen Carson Schatz joined Combs/fiddle, Mike Compton/mandolin, Chris on guitar, Mark Schatz on bass, and me playing banjo for fifteen compositions from the John Hartford catalogue. Three ("Madison, Tennessee," "Homer the Roamer," and "She's Gone [And Bob's Gone with Her"]) were leftovers from the aborted *Old Family Jig* rehearsals. Two of Ed Haley's fiddle tunes ("Three Forks of Sandy" and "Half Past Four") John had recorded for *The Speed of the Old Long Bow*. A pair of Hartford performances were from demos provided by his estate. The remainder we had played many times onstage during those last years of John's life. The resulting disc was released in Japan by Red Clay Records and in the rest of the world by Compass. It was nominated for a Grammy.

John had requested that his archive be kept together after his death. Recreating John's office as a whole entity, however, proved impractical. Therefore, parts of his collection were thematically dispersed by John's children to various existing institutions. Steamboat-related materials went to the Mercantile Library at the University of Missouri-St. Louis; music books to Vanderbilt's Blair School of Music; recordings to the Center for Popular Music at Middle Tennessee State University; and memorabilia, photographs, and the like to the Country Music Foundation in Nashville.

Fiddler Matt Combs and Greg Reish of the Center for Popular Music assisted John's daughter Katie in assembling a book of his original tunes for the fiddle. *John Hartford's Mammoth Collection of Fiddle Tunes* (2018) was just one of the posthumous projects published by the John Hartford estate after his passing.

Thanks for letting us stand on your stage.

When I began working alongside John Hartford, I thought I knew something about music and performing. It turns out that I only knew a fraction of what I was about to learn in his musical workshop. I came out the other end a much better entertainer and musician than before my experience with John.

John's shows were unpredictable. He would read the audience to determine what he felt he needed to perform in that moment. John had such a large repertoire that you didn't know what he'd play for any particular performance. Each night, there would always be a song or two that the band didn't know. Playing with John was always one big experimental continuum. Everyone involved, if they left themselves open, always learned something new. And that was the whole point.

I don't think John cared that mass taste was different from his taste. John didn't want to be like everybody else. That would have been boring.

Before playing with John, I had all these unconnected ideas about how to take the old-time clawhammer style of banjo playing and make it my own. I wanted to be unique yet traditional, crafting a cohesive approach that would fit with any style of music. Within the Hartford Stringband, John allowed me the freedom to develop my approach, to take bits and pieces from various places and come up with something new and personal to fit his situation.

John challenged me with music that I would not have normally chosen to play. He encouraged me to try to come up with a successful method to perform his repertoire, and to develop my own interactive banjo style.

John was good at pushing you, knocking you off balance, and watching to see how you would recover. He'd do that both on stage and in the studio, as well as in everyday situations. John would throw you a solo in a place that you didn't expect it in a song that you'd never played just to see what you could come up with.

Those are my biggest memories of him.

John, understandably, fought his inevitable demise when it was staring him in the face. While he was still mentally able, he tried to process the end-of-life experience. When John began to see the tunnel's light up ahead, he came up with several scenarios for his transition.

John once told me that he wanted to be buried in his tour bus. "Just dig a big hole," John said, "and drive the bus in." On another occasion, John informed his audience:

> Let me tell you something now. When and if [I die], and it is inevitable, I'm going to have myself blown up. I'd get into the car, load it all down with song lyrics, bills, statements and all that

crap and wire it. Put the wire back there in a field and have the preacher get back there, have everybody come sit in the bleachers, and have a funeral service. And, at the end of the prayer, the preacher pushes the plunger, blam! you'd have a whole sky full of mementos.

Otherwise, I thought, if I had myself cremated, I'd have all the ashes split up and do a mailing [to radio stations], saying, "Thanks for the spin."

Thanks for the spin, John. The ride was bumpy, unpredictable, challenging, frightening, but also enlightening, joyous, and fulfilling. We all miss you. The world could sure use you back.

Afterlife

When It's Over, It's Just Over

David Holt interviewed John in 1996 and had him describe John's thoughts about his cancer and death:

> I just finally figured out that, when it's over, it's just over. And all your need to prove yourself, to eat, to establish your territory . . . is no longer there. And it has to be the most wonderful, relaxing sleep that you can possibly imagine. So, when I think of it that way, when I get to the end of line, it's gonna be the desert of the most amazing quality possible. That takes a lot of the fear and burden out of it.

Mike Compton recalls that John once told him that he didn't believe in an afterlife, that a person's energy just disperses and goes out into the universe. If so, it took a while for such a strong force of nature to disappear. I was not alone in experiencing the night visitations by John that began immediately following John's exit from this mortal coil.

In my dreams (if they were indeed dreams), I would open my eyes and see a figure in silhouette standing in front of the closed door to my room. I might call out something like "what do you want?" but, never received an answer. Eventually, I'd close my eyes and go back to sleep. Those visitations have since ceased. However, I'll often, especially when John is in the front of my consciousness, such as when I've been writing this book, have dreams where John is alive and healthy and either making music or crewing on a riverboat. I'm always surprised that he's survived, and, that I'm not a part of his current group or endeavors.

Matt Combs also was paid a visit by John, prompting some of the words to a new song, "John, Bring That Fiddle 'Round." When Matt told me this story, I was motivated to help him finish the composition:

On the Cumberland River, where the muddy waters flow,
Lived an old riverman that played the banjo,
He wore a derby hat so everyone would know,
His show had come to town
The old fiddle tunes, and the new ones too,
The songs that he wrote, doodle, oodle, ooh,
He'd sing and he'd dance for me and for you,
Thank you very much

Chorus:

John, bring that fiddle 'round
John, his show has come to town
John, making those rafters ring
All join hands and circle to the left
And form a great big ring.

The Julia Belle Swain, Gentle on My Mind
It's Natural to Be Gone
Bring Your Clothes Back Home, Aereo Plane
Don't Leave Your Records in the Sun
Here's to Your Dreams, I'm Still Here
You and Me at Home
Vamp in the Middle, Presbyterian Guitar
Turn Your Radio On

John, Skippin' in the Mississippi Dew
John, The Steamboat Whistle Blues
John, There'll Never Be Another You

We're Learning to Smile All Over Again in the old Gum Tree
*   Canoe*

It's been a few years since he's been gone, to join his friends on high
We planted him next to the Cumberland River
Just to hear those boats go by
We miss him so
But we know he's alright
Because we hear his old fiddle out on the river
When we're staying up late at night

John, he's playin' in the heavenly band
John, with Benny Martin close at hand
John, with Roy Huskey as his guide
Ed Haley, Bill Monroe, and his mom and dad
Have joined him on the other side.

Selected Bibliography

Ancestry.com.

Bruton, Elizabeth. "Hartford's talent, versatility result in a wonderful show." *Charlotte Observer*, April 12, 1996.

Buckingham, Bob. *Fiddler Magazine* 3, no. 1 (Spring 1996).

Carlin, Bob. Archive of materials pertaining to my fifteen-year friendship with John Hartford, including live recordings, calendar books, publicity materials, recording session tapes and notes, photographs, reviews, and correspondence, among other documentation.

Carlin, Bob. "Interview with John Hartford." *Fresh Air*. WHYY-FM, August 23, 1985.

Coole, Chris. *Old Time News* 107 (Autumn 2021).

Coulson, Steve. "Nitty Gritty Band was worth waiting for." *Manhattan Mercury*, February 16, 1975.

Davis, John T. "Reticent guitar star lets music speak for him." *Austin American-Statesman*, January 18, 1985.

"Gentle Struggle for Perfection." New York Times News Service, *Minneapolis Star Tribune*, February 8, 2000.

Gillespie, Gail. "Bob Carlin—Capped Crusader for Old-Time Music." *Old Time Herald* 7, no. 3 (Fall 2000).

Hartford, John. *John Hartford's Mammoth Collection of Fiddle Tunes*.

"Interview with John Hartford." *David Holt's State of Music*. YouTube, 1996.

John Hartford website. 2018. johnhartford.com.

Menius, Art. "John Hartford as I Knew Him." Academia.edu. https://www.academia .edu/21657849/John_Hartford_As_I_Knew_Him.

The Mississippi: River of Song. Smithsonian/PBS, 1998.

Moss-Cohane, Marty. "Interview with John Hartford." *Radio Times* WHYY-FM, 1988.

Newspapers.com.

Piazza, Tom. Booklet notes for *Good Old Boys*. CD, Rounder Records, 1999.

Rice, Gary. "Hartford Dazzles Audience." *Kansas City Star*, November 18, 1979.

SELECTED DISCOGRAPHY:
JOHN HARTFORD AND BOB CARLIN

1991: *The Civil War Music Collector's Edition*—Time-Life Music
1995: *The Fun of Open Discussion*—Rounder Records
1996: *Wild Hog in the Red Brush*—Rounder Records
1997–1998: *Ed Haley*—Rounder Records
1998: *The Speed of the Old Long Bow*—Rounder Records
1999: *The Banjo According to John Hartford*—Homespun Tapes
1999: *Good Old Boys*—Rounder Records
2001: *Hamilton Ironworks*—Rounder Records
2001: *Gum Tree Canoe*—Flying Fish Records
2002: *Steam Powered Aereo-Takes*—Rounder Records

INDEX

Page numbers in *italics* refer to images.

Acuff, Charlie, 46
Acuff, Roy, 36
Akeman, Dave "Stringbean," 4
Akimoto, Shin, 58, *59*
Atkins, Chet, 12
Axton, Hoyt, 16

Barrett, Susan Marie Fielder, 26, 31, 34,
    36, 40, 42, 48, 50, 61, 62, 65, 66, 68,
    70, 74, 75, 78, 82, 89–90, 109, 113, 125,
    127, 128, 130
Berline, Byron Douglas, 16, 44–45, 108
Berry, Chuck, 105
Best, Carroll, 46
Bird, Elmer, 35
Blake, Norman, 17–18, 19–20, 22, 122, 123
Blye, Allan, 15
Boatwright, Ginger, 107
Book Binder, Roy, 62
Bromberg, David, 19, 40, 97, 111, 122
Brown, Alison, 35, 107, 132
Brown, Don, 10, 105
Bub, Mike, *88*, 89
Buckner, George, 132
Burnett, T Bone, 131
Bush, Sam, 17, 122, 130, 131
Byrds, 16

Campbell, Glen, 14, 15, 16, 17, 38, 60, 79
Carl, George, 23

Carroll, Lewis, 45, 97
Case, Keith, 20, 45, 48, 82, 105
Chancellor, James David "Texas Shorty,"
    41, 43–45, 118
Clapton, Eric, 79
Clement, Jack, 32–33, 34, 35, 40, 47, 79,
    92, 94
Clements, Vassar, 16, 18, 19, 25, 122
Coen, Joel and Ethan, 113–14
Combs, Matt, 3, 93, 115, 124, 125, *126*,
    131–32, 136
Compton, Michael Curtis "Mike,"
    42, 61–62, 64, 70, 72, *73*, 74, 81, *84*,
    84–86, 88, *88*, 93, *94*, 95, 96, 98, 104,
    105, 107, 108, 111, 112, 113, 114, 115, *115*,
    116, *117*, 118, 120, 122, *123*, 124, 125, 131,
    132, 135
Cowan, John, 123

Davis, Nawana, 20
Delaney and Bonnie, 16
Didlake, Scott, 36
Dillard, Douglas, 7, 10, 16, 25, 121
Dillard, Homer, 7, 46, 121
Dillard, Rodney, 7, 25, 121
Dillards, the, 16, 45
Douglas, Jerry, 130
Douglas, Wilson, 69
Dunn, Louie, 46

Einstein, Bob, 15
Elliot, Ramblin' Jack, 122
Elza, Charles "Kentucky Slim," 6
Emmons, Buddy, 77

Ferris, Ruth, 8–9, 25
Flatt & Scruggs, 5–6, 12, 33, 42, 92, 108, 112
Fleck, Bela, 35, 85, 123, 132
Flynn, Pat, 123
Ford, Norman, 10, 105
Forester, Howdy, 46
Franklin, Major, 46

Gately, Robert, 81
Glaser, Chuck, 11, 13–14, 16
Glaser, Jim, 11
Glaser, Tompall, 11, 110
Glaser Brothers publishing, 26
Glasser, Dave, 70
Goforth, Cecil, 115
Goforth, Gene, 46, 80, 115, 121
Gottlieb, Carl, 15
Gray, Dr., 4
Grey, Adie, 77
Grier, David, 42, 108
Grisman, David, 103, 130
Gruhn, George, 18, 78–79, 128

Haley, Alex, 41
Haley, James Edward "Ed," 37, 47, 67–70, 71, 80, 81, 82, 85, 111, 122, 132, 137
Haley, Lawrence, 68, 69, 70, 80
Harford, Betty L. Beck, 11, 41, 107
Harford, Carl Gayler, 3, 26, 116, 118
Harford, James Cowan "Jamie," 11, 34, 41, 49, 70, 72, 97, 105, 123, 131
Harford, Kathryn Gayler "Katie," 11, 41, 132
Harford, Mary Broadhead Cowan, 3, 4, 5–6, 26, 27, 75
Harris, Emmylou, 130

Haven, Kate, and Stoner, 7
Hawthorne, Marvin, and Clifford, 10
Holland, Dave, 25, 122
Holt, David, 26–27, 65, 113, 135
Hotze, John, 131
Howard, Harlan, 42, 98–99
Howard, Jan, 14
Howard, Mark, 32, 33, 34, 39, 40, 46, 47, 71, 72, 73, 79, 81, 96
Huskey, Roy, Jr., 34, 40, 49, 72, 84, 108, 137
Hutson, Joe, 61

Irwin, John Rice, 41
Irwin, Ken, 110

Jackson, Roger, 61
Johnson, Jimmy, 61–62, 90, 109
Jones, Nelson, 109

Kinslow, Lem, 61
Kirk, Brandon, 67–70
Knuckles, Ray, 46

Lachot, Wes, 81, 99, 120
Lewis, Henry, 93
Lewis sisters ("Miggie," Polly, and Janis), 109–10
Libbea, Gene, 89

Mace, Lee, 7
Macon, Uncle Dave, 30, 47
Martin, Benny, 5–6, 12, 16, 25, 42, 76, 116, 123, 137
Martin, Dan, 8
Martin, Jimmy, 36
Martin, Steve, 15
Mattea, Kathy, 123
Matthews, William, 130
McCoury, Del, 61, 70, 89, 116, 122
McCoury, Jerry, 61–62, 70, 73, 74, 112
McCoury, Ronnie, 70, 72, 89

McGuiness, Ruth, 34
Miller, Roger, 77
Minner, Calvin, 35
Monroe, Bill, 6, 35, 42, 73, 78, 86, 96, 112, 116, 123, 137
Moss, Frazier, 39
Music, Jerry, 15

Nash, Ogden, 30, 45, 97
Nelson, Curly, 10
Nelson, Jim, 7, 120
Nelson, Tim Blake, 113
Nemerov, Bruce, 39, 70
Nickel Creek, 127

O'Brien, Tim, 85, 123, 130, 132
O'Bryant, Alan, 39, 132
O'Bryant, Dale, 38–39
O'Connor, Mark, 16, 39, 59, 67
Odell, Holly, 34
Ohmori, Yasuhiro "Taco," 55
Osborne, Sonny, 78
Osborne Brothers, 77, 119, 130
Oster, Fred, 79

Pacheco, Tom, 16
Perkins, Larry, 61–62, 63, 64, 77, 84–85, 87, 93, 95, 99, 104, 105, 111, 112, 113, 114, 115, 116, 117, 118, 119, 120, 121, 123, 125, 126, 131
Persinger, Cleo, 44–45
Phillips, Bruce "Utah," 122
Phillips, Todd, 73, 127

Queen, Roy, 5

Reiner, Rob, 15
Rice, Tony, 85, 122
Roberts, "Doc," 46

Sasabe, Masuo, 51, 54, 54–55
Saul, Bernie, 48, 65, 82

Scancarelli, Jim, 8
Schatz, Eileen Carson, 132
Schatz, Mark, 84, 84–85, 89, 94, 95, 97, 98, 99, 132
Scott, Darrell, 130
Scrivenor, Gove, 16
Scruggs, Earl, 4, 5–6, 12, 19–20, 40, 43, 73, 76, 77, 91–92, 93, 112, 116, 119, 123, 130
Scruggs, Louise, 43
Seals and Crofts, 16
Seckler, Curly, 6
Seeger, Mike, 103, 105
Sharp, Larry Christopher "Chris," 59, 64, 84, 84, 85, 86, 87, 88, 91, 92–95, 94, 98, 103, 104, 111, 112, 114, 115, 116, 117, 118, 120, 123, 125, 126, 128, 130, 131
Sims, Benny, 67
Sinclair, Cindy, 130
Smothers, Dick, 15, 16, 17
Smothers, Tommy, 14–15, 16, 17, 23
Smothers Brothers, 14, 15, 17, 29, 30, 60, 79
Snider, Mike, 131
Stevenson, McLean, 15
Stinnett, Cyril, 46
Stubbs, Eddie, 130
Swift, Jimmy, 89

Takaki, "Bosco," 57, 59
Taylor, James, 16
Taylor, Kate, 16
Taylor, Robert Arthur "Tut," 17–18, 19, 122
Thiele, Chris, 122, 127
Thomas, Guthrie, 16
Thompson, Bill, 14
Traum, Happy, 91, 92, 129

Van Dyke, Leroy, 62
Vincent, Darrin, 61–62, 73, 81

Welch, Gillian and David Rawlings, 105, 123, 130

Wells, Paul, 39–40

Wendt, Tim, 61

Whelan, Johnny, 46

Williams, Mason, 14–15

Wolfe, Charles, 120

Wood, Jim, 80

Wooliver, Roy, 121

Woolsey, Diddie, 9

Yudkin, Jonathan, 34, 40

ABOUT THE AUTHOR

YOU'LL BE USED TO HIM BY THE END OF THE SET,
BY JOHN HARTFORD AND DAN LEVENSON

Bob has been very [fortunate], if you will, to have played with some great musicians. John Hartford is certainly among the best of them. But, I think, John had a stroke of genius when he decided to have Bob Carlin play banjo for him in those last years before John passed away.

—DAN LEVENSON

Bob Carlin is the most famous guy in the band, including the leader. He's the first in recent times to really make a drop thumb banjo style fit into a contemporary old-time band style. He understands old-time country music better than most people who come from that in their background and brings an Eastern sophistication to it that these old country boys sometimes can't quite get their teeth around—certainly a rare combination. He produces our records and gets a freshness out of us that we can't seem to get any other way. He's great on the road, he takes care of everything from visiting with [banjo collector and historian] Jim Bollman and seeing instruments we never thought we'd see for real to finding the best sushi restaurants. He's funny, he keeps us laughing all the time; we can argue and yell and come away friends. He's a collector of vintage clothing, and he got [Hartford Stringband member] Chris Sharp the finest shoes you ever saw.

Above all and most important, he's a fine musician and understands time and intonation really well. He's also a good singer and creative with his own work which we try to feature every show, and has a great voice, although he doesn't think so. He's a fine writer and has written many great magazine articles. Sometimes when he's out on the road with us, he lets us tag along when he goes to do his research. He has a cell phone, and we can reach him any time of day or night, which is really neat. In addition to being a fine record producer he really knows about microphones and all the sophisticated electronics that go into all that. He did a superb job on the Ed Haley reissues [which John produced for Rounder Records] in addition to proof-reading our liner notes. We all love him and hope he'll stay with us for a long time.

—JOHN HARTFORD

Milton Keynes UK
Ingram Content Group UK Ltd.
UKHW031305260824
1385UKWH00041B/340

9 781496 851390